Reaching Out, Joining In

Teaching Social Skills to Young Children with Autism

Topics in Autism

Reaching Out, Joining In

Teaching Social Skills to Young Children with Autism

Mary Jane Weiss, Ph.D., BCBA &
Sandra L. Harris, Ph.D.

Woodbine House ◆ 2001

All rights reserved under International and Pan-American copyright conventions. Published in the United States of America by Woodbine House, Inc., 6510 Bells Mill Rd., Bethesda, MD 20817. 800-843-7323. www.woodbinehouse.com

Library of Congress Cataloging-in-Publication Data

Gill-Weiss, Mary Jane.
    Reaching out, joining in : teaching social skills to young children with autism / by Mary Jane Weiss, Sandra L. Harris.—1ˢᵗ ed.
        p. cm. – (Topics in autism.)
    Includes bibliographical references and index.
        ISBN 1-890627-24-0 (paper)
        1.Autistic children—Rehabilitation. 2. Autistic children—Education. 3. Social skills in children. 4. Autistic children—Behavior modification. 5. Behavior assessment. I. Harris, Sandra L. II. Title. III. Series

RJ506.A9 G53 2001
618.92'898203—dc21

                                                                                    2001025836

Manufactured in the United States of America

First edition
10 9 8 7 6 5 4 3

In Celebration of Our Brothers

In Memory of Bill Coneys and in
Honor of Jay Harris

And in celebration of siblings everywhere who
love their brothers and sisters with autism and
bring so much to that special relationship.

TABLE OF CONTENTS

INTRODUCTION

The technical know-how for treating children with autism is more sophisticated and effective today than at any time in the history of the field. Unfortunately, we have not yet become effective at disseminating this knowledge to every family who needs it.

To help remedy the information vacuum, we have written this book to share with parents and professionals what we have learned about teaching social skills to children with autism. In this book, we use the term "autism" to refer to children with Autistic Disorder, Asperger's Disorder (also known as Asperger syndrome), and Pervasive Developmental Disorder Not Otherwise Specified (PDDNOS).

Although this book is written primarily for parents, we expect that classroom teachers, speech-language pathologists, and home consultants will find some of the ideas in this book useful as well. Many of our colleagues have told us they found the suggestions helpful in developing instructional programs in their classroom or as part of a home program.

Our recommendations for teaching social skills come from our understanding of the professional literature and from our own combined forty-five years of testing these methods in our work with families. We know these methods have been effective for some children because we have measured their progress and tracked their outcome over the years. We also recognize that what works well for some youngsters has much more limited value for others. Although our ability to teach social skills is at an all-time high, it falls short of the goal of universal benefits to which we aspire. There is still much research to be done.

The mastery of social skills is one of the most daunting challenges facing people with autism. Even youngsters whose academic skills are at grade level and who are capable of sophisticated language report how difficult it is for them to read and use the social cues in their environment. We both know many youngsters who are functioning well academically in a regular classroom but who are on the periphery of the social life of their classmates. Some of these children may benefit considerably from the systematic approach to teaching social skills we describe in our book. Yet, even mastery of every skill covered in this book will still leave many children in need of continuing help in the development of social relationships. Learning how to teach social and emotional skills to people with autism remains one of the major challenges in our field. We hope the next decade will see significant changes in those limits.

We have not written this book solely for those children who will make rapid and relatively easy progress through the programs. Although some children may learn more slowly and be more limited in their ultimate progress, there is reason to expect that most children with autism can learn some of these skills. In general, however, children who have more language and learn other skills more quickly will move through these programs faster than children who have little language and for whom all learning comes more slowly.

About This Book

Our goal in this book is to introduce readers to social skills programs for preschool and elementary school aged children with autism. By "programs," we mean detailed descriptions of how to teach specific activities such as how to shoot baskets or recognize jokes. Most of the research on basic play has been done with young children for whom play is a primary mode of expression. A creative teacher or parent may be able to adapt these concepts for older children, but you should take care to use age-appropriate materials. For example, a pre-teen would use sports equipment or video games rather than dolls or trucks to engage another child.

Our approach to teaching social skills relies upon the use of applied behavior analysis (ABA). As we describe in Chapter 1, ABA involves a particular way of thinking about behavior change and uses a range of teaching tools, such as discrete trial instruction (DTI), methods of motivating children to work hard at learning, a system for understanding disruptive behavior such as tantrums, and advanced teaching techniques including modeling, role plays, and social scripts. We will discuss these methods in some detail in Chapter 1 and throughout the book.

We will focus our attention on how to teach skills in four broad domains. The first is play, one of the most important activities of childhood. Through their play children learn the practical "physics" of how objects respond when they are manipulated, they learn how to share attractive toys or activities with one another, they try on different social roles, and they sometimes process events that have special meaning for them. Chapter Two describes ways to introduce your child to basic play skills.

Chapter Three addresses how to teach what we call the "language of social skills." This "language" includes an appreciation of the basic rules of getting along with other children. To be an acceptable playmate, a child must follow the basics of childhood relationships such as not hitting another child to get his own way. He must learn to share information with another child and ask for what he needs to know; for example, telling another child "It's your turn," or "I need the wheel." We also address some of the basic gestures a child needs to communicate well with another child. For example, being able to give a "high five" may be very important for fitting in with other children. A number of conversational skills are introduced in Chapter Three. These include knowing childhood slang, telling jokes, responding to other people's conversational efforts, and sustaining a conversation over time.

In Chapter Four, we turn our attention to programs to help a child with autism adopt another person's perspective. The term "perspective taking" refers to the ability to empathize with another person, or "stand in his shoes." People with autism, whether children or adults, typically have a great deal of trouble understanding how another person's point of view may differ from their own. Chapter Four briefly describes some research on perspective taking in autism and suggests some teaching programs to help your child improve in this domain.

Chapter Five describes ways to help children with autism transfer their skills into a classroom with typically developing peers. We consider the skills that can best be taught in a group setting and some programs for teaching these skills. We also discuss the roles to be filled by the teacher, by a special coach for the child with autism called a "shadow," by typically developing peers, and by the child with autism. If you are a parent, this chapter may help you identify the skills your child needs to function well in an included setting and give you some ideas about how to evaluate these settings. If you are a teacher, the chapter will help you think about how to adapt your curriculum to increase social interactions among your students.

Thirty years ago, it would have been impossible to write a book like ours. The field of applied behavior analysis had just been launched and we were only beginning to learn how to teach such fundamentals as clapping hands and getting dressed. Thanks to that research-based foundation built by a whole community of scientists and practitioners, we are now able to focus on the much subtler and very important challenge of teaching children with autism the social skills they need to be more fully a part of the community of childhood.

Mary Jane Weiss & Sandra L. Harris
March 2001

ACKNOWLEDGEMENTS

We are deeply indebted to our many colleagues at the Douglass Developmental Disabilities Center and the Rutgers Autism Program, whose technical sophistication, passion, and creativity have made a profound difference in the lives of children with autism and their families. Our thanks to Maria Arnold, Lara Delmolino, Lew Gantwerk, Peter Gerhardt, Beth Glasberg, Rita Gordon, Jan S. Handleman, Barbara Kristoff, and Ellen Yeagle for all they have taught us over the years. A special thanks is extended to the members of the Rutgers Autism Program staff who have contributed to the development of the curricular progressions and clinical procedures described in this book. In particular, we acknowledge the significant contributions of Matthew Bowman, Beth Glasberg, Noel Nelson, Kendra Peacock, and Jacqueline Wright of the Rutgers Autism Program and Lara Delmolino of the Douglass Developmental Disabilities Center. Jean Burton, professor emeritus in psychology at Rutgers University, was instrumental in the founding of the Douglass Center and both of us owe her thanks.

Much of what we have learned as professionals we have learned from and with the children and families whom we have served. We are grateful to them for all they have taught us and for the trust they have placed in us.

Mary Jane thanks her mother, Joan Coneys, for her wisdom and example. Mary Jane is forever grateful to and indebted to Danny for his infinite support, humor, love, and friendship. And a special thank you goes to Liam, who personifies hope and is an endless source of happiness, joy, and laughter to his parents and to all who know and love him.

Sandra thanks her niece, Ilona, nephew, Gary, and their children, Emma and Molly, for the happiness they bring to her days. Thanks also to Joseph Masling, whose mentorship made her a psychologist, and to Han van den Blink, who helped her recognize the joy in her life.

1 | Social Skills: Ways to Learn and Things to Teach

Allison Kimball watched her three-year-old son, Scott, with mixed emotions. She was proud of the progress he had made since they had started treatment for his autism, and dismayed by everything yet to be learned.

A year ago, Scott had been diagnosed as having Autistic Disorder. At that time he was not speaking and he often seemed to be off in his own little dream world. Although he accepted their hugs, he did not seem very aware of his parents, and he was oblivious to his older sister, Rita. What seemed to please Scott the most was lining up his toy cars and walking around them in a circle. If he did not have his cars, sticks would do as well.

When Allison and her husband, Jack, had described their son's behavior at home, the pediatrician had recognized the seriousness of Scott's behavior. She had referred the Kimballs to a nearby medical center, where a full work-up led to the diagnosis. Although the diagnosis plunged them into a state of emotional tumult, they wasted little time finding out what to do for their boy. Within a few weeks after the diagnosis, the Kimballs were immersed in a home-based ABA program for two-year-old Scott.

The home program had already done wonders. Scott had a growing vocabulary and was putting words into two- and sometimes three-word combinations. He followed a number of simple directions, imitated just about any gesture that was modeled by his teachers, and could sort objects by their color, size, shape, or basic functions. (For instance, he could put the pictures of foods in one pile and the toys in another.) It was thrilling to watch their son make progress. In spite of *the good news, Scott still had autism. This was most evident in how he got along, or more precisely, did not get along with other people. His play skills were very limited, he showed no interest in "Let's pretend," and he remained oblivious to children.*

It broke Allison's heart to watch her daughter try to get Scott to play. Rita, who was five years old, would approach Scott and show him a toy or invite him to join her in what she was doing. He would simply ignore her, and if she pressed, he screamed until she left him alone. Rita would look crestfallen, and, Allison realized, had lately almost stopped trying to get Scott's attention. It wasn't an easy situation to explain to a five-year-old.

Allison and Jack had shared these concerns with Matt Becker, their home consultant. Matt was a superb teacher who had helped the Kimballs create a high quality home program. Every six weeks he visited their home for a day, reviewing new programs, demonstrating teaching methods, and evaluating Scott's progress. In between visits they spoke to Matt on the phone every week, and sometimes they sent him videotapes. When Allison brought up her concerns about Scott's failure to play and lack of interest in other children, Matt agreed that it was a good time to address those skills. Scott followed directions, cooperated during teaching sessions, and engaged in fewer stereotypic behaviors such as hand waving and rocking than he had early in treatment. All of these new skills, along with his increasingly complex speech, laid the groundwork for helping Scott become more social.

Matt told the Kimballs that teaching play and other social behaviors would proceed much like Scott's other programs. They would start with basic building-block skills and elaborate these into more complex behaviors. Scott would have to learn how to take turns, to follow simple rules, and to pretend. For example, before he could share a toy with another child, he would have to learn to manipulate the toy. He could not "play hospital" with his sister if he did not understand what to do with a toy stethoscope.

As Matt explained, first Allison or Jack would be Scott's play partners. Once Scott had some basic competence, Rita could be his partner. The children's games at first might consist of rolling a ball or giving hugs. Later they would share toys and begin to pretend with toys. Scott would also learn to imitate the things Rita did and to take turns with her. Big gains could come from small steps.

Are Your Concerns Like the Kimballs'?

If you are the parent of a child with autism, or a teacher or speech-language therapist who works with these children, the Kimballs' story is probably familiar to you. Your child may be very much like Scott, or quite different, but in any case you too are undoubtedly challenged by your child's social problems. Deficits in social skills are part of the diagnosis of autism. Whether your child has Autistic Disorder, Asperger's Disorder, or Pervasive Developmental Disorder Not Otherwise Specified, problems in social relatedness are among his challenges.

Perhaps your child, like Scott, has learned some good basic cognitive and speech skills but is still socially isolated. Or, perhaps your child has good language and shows an awareness of other children, but is baffled as to how to join them in their play. Or, maybe your child is less aware of other people than Scott is and has not yet developed any speech.

Regardless of your child's current abilities, you no doubt want him to become more skillful in relating to other people. The techniques of applied behavior analysis (ABA) that the Kimball family used for Scott are helpful for most children on the autism spectrum. This book will introduce you to ABA techniques that are useful in establishing social behavior. We will also describe some specific teaching programs that may be helpful for your child.

What Do We Mean by Development?

Watching the unfolding of a child's development is usually one of the joys of parenthood. By "development" we are referring to a combination of biological changes and learning experiences

that result in a child acquiring increasingly complex skills. Children develop skills in many different areas, including speech and language, motor, and social skills.

The process of human development has not only been a source of fascination and joy for parents, it has been the subject of scientific study for many years. Through careful observation of babies, children, teens, and adults, we have learned to understand the many developmental changes that occur over time.

One of the things we have observed is the wide variation in typical development. We know that some children talk "early" and others are "late." While the typical child walks with his hand held at twelve months, some will do this a couple of months earlier, and some a few months later. The same child who walks earlier may speak later or earlier than the average. All of these variations are "normal." It is only when a child is very late in reaching a developmental milestone that we grow concerned. It was probably your child's significant delays in speech and in social awareness that first caught your attention and led you to raise questions with your pediatrician.

If you have other children, or if you know other young children such as cousins or youngsters in the neighborhood, you may have recognized fairly early that there was something unusual about your child's development. You knew how old your typically developing daughter was when she started to speak, and how she was fascinated with your face and took comfort from your presence, even at an early age. Your son with autism may not have started to speak on time, and even as a baby may not have seemed as interested in you as your daughter was. Because your daughter had taught you about typical development, it was easier to see that your son's development was different. If you have no other children, it may have taken you a bit longer to recognize that your child's development was unusual.

A clear example of typical development is seen in how children learn motor skills. These skills follow some basic patterns. One pattern is that they develop from top to bottom. We can manipulate objects with our hands before we can walk. A second pattern is that our movements grow more precise. The very young child grabs an object with her whole hand. A somewhat older child uses her thumb and forefinger to pick up a tiny object. Table 1-1 illustrates a few of the major developmental milestones that occur as we develop our gross (large muscle) and fine (small muscle) motor control.

Children with autism typically show considerable developmental variation among their skills in different areas. For example, their motor skills are usually less delayed than speech and language or social skills. Unfortunately, however, if your child has good abilities in one domain (such as fine motor skills), it does

---

Table 1-1 | The Development of Gross and Fine Motor Skills

Skill	Average Age
Sits erect indefinitely	10 Months
Walks with one hand held	12 Months
Uses finger-thumb pincer grasp	12 Months
Walks upstairs, one hand held	18 Months
Kicks ball	24 Months
Turns page	24 Months
Alternates feet going upstairs	36 Months
Rides tricycle	36 Months
Alternates feet walking downstairs	48 Months
Skips	60 Months

not mean that he can also be expected to show similar abilities in another area such as speech. And delays your child has in one area can affect development of skills in another. For instance, a child whose gross and fine motor skills are delayed will have a hard time learning social games that require him to run, jump, or throw a ball. Similarly, a child whose language is limited will encounter considerable challenges in learning social skills that are dependent upon speech.

What About Social Development?

Social development, like motor development, follows a general pattern of growth. Consider, for example, how we leave another person. At ten months of age, a child may wave bye-bye when a guest leaves. The two-year-old may say "bye-bye" or may be too shy to say anything when leaving. An older child may plan where and when he will see his friend again before leaving. For an adolescent or adult, the process of leave-taking can range from a formal handshake and the scheduling of a next meeting, to a hug or a long discussion as dear friends part. The older we get, the more nuanced our leaving behavior becomes.

Although all of the love, nurture, guidance, and care parents provide is certainly crucial to healthy development of social skills, some of a child's social abilities seem to unfold almost effortlessly. Children seem "pre-programmed" to love their parents, cuddle, play with toys, and enjoy pretending to be cowhands or astronauts.

We know biology plays a key role in social skills development because parents of children with autism, like most parents everywhere, love their babies, cuddle them, sing to them, and stimulate them with toys. In spite of this loving care, the child with autism does not develop the social awareness and skills that seem to come so easily to most children.

When a baby is developing typically, an interest in other people is present from his earliest days. Even at two months of age, infants find the human face more interesting to look at than other kinds of images. Another person's eyes are a special focus of attention for a baby. Babies seem to be "programmed" to smile in the presence of a human face. Tiny babies also have the capacity to imitate the simple motor movements of another person, including opening their mouths or moving their fingers.

Babies show a special attachment to their caregivers. They are upset when separated from a parent and comforted when a parent returns. Separation distress, a tearful reaction by children when a parent leaves, reaches its peak around one year of age, but can be observed as early as nine months of age, when some children become fearful of strangers. This attachment to parents is shown in other ways. It is visible in the young child's healthy pleasure at being in the room with a parent and his delight in exploring when he knows his parents are nearby and he can periodically return to them. That ritual of wandering away and then returning is important in learning to feel secure on one's own.

This interest in other people is not confined to parents. Even babies show a special interest in other children, and the preschool aged child spends much of his time learning the give-and-take of play with other children. We will discuss the process of typical social development in each chapter as background for understanding the skills your child needs to become a more socially competent person.

What about Social Skills in Autism?

The development of social skills in children with autism is quite different than in typically developing youngsters. The very young child with autism demonstrates little interest in other people. His attachment to his parents may be less obvious than the typical child's and he may show little or no separation distress. Although some children with autism show pleasure in being with a familiar adult, they usually have minimal or no interest in other children. Even those children who show an awareness of other youngsters appear baffled about how to approach them and join their play.

Another striking difference is in imitation skills. Young children generally like to imitate things that adults do. Pretending to use an electric razor like Daddy or to use a screwdriver to fix a toy like Mommy is one of the pleasures of small children. Have you ever seen a little boy walk down the street with the same swaggering gait as his father? That kind of imitation occurs spon-

taneously in typically developing children. By contrast, children with autism often have to be taught simple imitations such as clapping hands or standing up.

Similarly, although children with autism may engage in solitary play, especially with toys such as blocks or puzzles, they show little if any inclination to initiate playful interactions with other children. Additionally, their solitary play seldom has the free-flowing, creative quality of the typical child's, but is often more stereotypic or repetitive in nature. Scott Kimball, for example, would have been content to spend much of his time lining up toy cars in the same repetitive pattern and then walking around them in a circle. By contrast, a typically developing child might line up his cars to race around a track.

His play would probably be filled with sound effects and dialog about the action at the racetrack.

Even among children with autism who engage in some imaginary play, the scenarios tend to be simple and repetitive, with none of the variation that is common in children their age. Typically developing children are capable of assuming a variety of roles and inventing scripts they never acted before. In contrast, children with autism may memorize a few roles, but have trouble inventing new ones. This limited capacity for fantasy is probably another reflection of their problems in social imagination and understanding the experiences of other people.

As you begin working with your child on social skills, it is important to realize that many children with autism initially take little pleasure in these skills. At first, you will have to support his early learning with a motivational (reward) system, as discussed below. However, most children will eventually feel genuine pleasure as they master the skills and enjoy other people's responses to them. Children who have the greatest difficulty absorbing information will need to be taught fewer rules of social behavior and be held to more flexible standards. Ultimately, however, many youngsters with autism will learn a broad range of social skills and function much like other children.

Teaching Methods

In this book, we approach the teaching of social skills from the perspective of applied behavior analysis (ABA). The term ABA refers to a special set of teaching tools that are especially useful in helping children with autism learn.

You may have heard of ABA in conjunction with one technique, called discrete trial instruction (DTI). In DTI a teacher presents an instruction to a child (for example, "touch your nose"), gives the child a chance to comply, and then rewards a correct response. Mistakes are corrected with redirection or they may be ignored, depending on the details of the child's teaching program.

When using DTI, it is important to try to end sessions on a positive note before the child gets frustrated, and to gradually increase the length of sessions. This instructional format is valuable for teaching some kinds of information such as imitating gestures or sounds, sorting objects, or obeying simple commands. For more information on the use of DTI, you can read our introductory book on ABA: *Right from the Start: Behavioral Intervention for Young Children with Autism* (Woodbine House, 1998).

Although DTI is perhaps the most common tool associated with ABA teaching, there are many others. In this book we will be applying a variety of ABA methods because many social behaviors are best taught by combining DTI with other ABA procedures. Table 1-2 lists some of the methods you will come upon in the next few chapters. We will describe these methods briefly here

---

Table 1-2 | Some ABA Teaching Methods

Motivating Behavior
- Reinforcement
- Incentive Systems
- Programming for Success

Shaping Behavior and Facilitating Generalization
- Shaping
- Chaining
- Programming for Generalization

Providing Models, Roles, Stories, and Scripts
- Modeling
- Observational Learning
- Analog Situations
- Role-Plays
- Social Stories

Naturalistic Instruction
- Incidental Teaching

and offer more information when they become relevant to the programs in later chapters.

Motivating Behavior

We all respond to some sort of incentive system when we work. Sometimes the incentive or "reinforcement" is something someone gives us. For example, you praise your child for carrying out the trash. Sometimes the reward is inherent in the activity. Play, for example, may be highly pleasurable in and of itself for typically developing children.

For children with autism, social situations are less motivating in and of themselves. As a result, you may have to create a special incentive system to motivate your child to learn social skills. Incentive systems can include stars on a chart or poker chips that can be traded for treats such as ice cream or extra TV time. Your child may have an incentive system as part of his home program or school program. This book cannot provide you all of the detail you may need to create an incentive system for your child. We suggest you speak with your child's teacher or home consultant if you need help motivating him to respond. For additional introductory information about incentive systems, take a look at a book by psychologists Bruce Baker and Alan Brightman, *Steps to Independence* (Paul Brookes, 1997). This book is also useful for teaching self-help skills.

It is important to understand that social interaction is work for most individuals with autism. Interacting with others is often not intrinsically rewarding for them, but instead, confusing and demanding. It is therefore essential that you identify effective rewards for your child. By "effective" rewards we mean those that can be shown to increase your child's learning. If he works hard for pickles, then these would be effective rewards. To judge whether a reward is effective, keep track of how much your child learns in a session. If he is learning new material, you have found a way to motivate him. Letting him choose his own rewards is also a good strategy.

Remember that reward selection is a highly individualized process. There are no universal reinforcers; many children enjoy rewards such as favorite play activities (e.g., being tossed in the air), a short break from work, or special foods. They can also usually learn to value opportunities to earn tokens or points that can be "cashed in" for desirable objects or activities. Nonetheless, what is an incentive for one child may not be for another. It is very important that you assess your child's preferences in order to identify rewards that will be effective.

There are a variety of methods for evaluating preferences. The behavior analyst working with your child should be able to guide this process. Teachers, school psychologists, and other specialists in educating children may all have helpful ideas about identifying reinforcers for your child. It is also important to recognize that reward preferences are quite dynamic. Preferences change from week to week, day to day, and moment to moment. Remember to assess your child's preferences on a continual basis to ensure that the rewards you are offering are currently effective motivators.

Another key principle of motivation in ABA teaching is to "program for success." It is important to arrange a lesson so that your child has a good chance of getting things right and few or no opportunities to make mistakes. The more often he makes correct responses and you can give him positive reinforcement for those behaviors, the faster he is likely to learn. Part of programming for success is breaking the task into small units and building one skill upon the next. The programs in this book aim to do that for you and your child. However, if the steps we describe are too big for your child, make them smaller. You need to adapt our programs to your own child.

Shaping Behavior and Facilitating Generalization

Other important aspects of teaching social behaviors are the shaping and chaining of behavior.

Shaping. Shaping is valuable in teaching play and social skills. When you shape a skill, you gradually refine it toward the precise response you have as your goal. For example, if you are teaching your child to throw a ball to you, you might begin by standing a foot apart and having him put the ball in your hands. Then you would move back a little, a little more, and a little more. Ultimately, you would stand several feet apart while he throws to you.

As shown in Table 1-3, several elements in a social interaction can be shaped, including the duration, reciprocity, and quality of the interaction between the children.

Shaping allows your child to learn a new skill by gradually building toward the identified goal. Using shaping will provide you with many opportunities to reinforce your child for the many small steps he takes toward a long-term goal.

Table 1-3 | Dimensions of Social Play

Duration—How long do they play?
Reciprocity—Is there a back and forth exchange between the children?
Quality—How age appropriate is the play?

Chaining. Chaining is the technical term to describe taking many small steps and combining them into a complex behavior. For example, if you wanted to teach your child to play a board game with another child, there are a number of skills that could be "chained" together. These include setting up the board, choosing a piece, rolling the dice, counting the spaces, taking turns, and so forth. You might start by teaching your child to set up the board on his own, then set up the board and choose his piece. Over time you would add more independent skills to the chain until he could play the entire game on his own. Using shaping and chaining effectively requires the help of an experienced person to teach you the methods. You should ask your child's teacher or a home consultant to help you master these ABA techniques.

Generalization. Children with autism often have problems transferring skills from one setting or one person to another. For example, a child may learn to play catch with his mother but not transfer that ability to another child. The process of transferring a skill from one place, object, or person to another is called generalization. Programming for generalization is an important aspect of teaching children with autism. The instructional programs in this book give suggestions for increasing the likelihood that your child can use his new skills with many different people and in different places and with a variety of toys or other objects. You should remember that generalization usually does not occur unless it is systematically addressed in the program.

Providing Models, Roles, Stories, and Scripts

Modeling. We often teach typically developing children by showing. Whether the skill is holding a baseball bat, apologizing for a mistake, or grasping a pen, we often show how it is done through our own behavior. This modeling of behavior is a powerful tool for teaching. However, it is only effective if the child is watching and motivated to do as we do. Learning through watching other people is called "observational learning." Observational learning occurs spontaneously in typically developing children, but often has to be taught to children with autism.

Another kind of modeling involves using the child himself as the model. Some children find it useful to see a videotape playback of themselves engaged in a behavior. You can coach your child in an appropriate response and show him the videotape of his performance, praising all he does right. We have some suggestions about how to make use of such visual feedback in Chapter Three.

Analog Situations. Sometimes teaching is best done in an artificial or sheltered situation that allows us to control some of the complexity of interactions that occur in the real world. We can use these so-called "analog situations" to introduce a child to new skills. (By analog, we mean an artificial situation that mimics a real one.) For example, if you want to teach your child to play baseball with other children, it would probably be too complex for him to go to a ballpark and play on a team of nine

children. Instead, your analog might involve having him play in the backyard with one other child. Similarly, if you want to place your child in a regular kindergarten, you might start with play sessions with one other child, then with a small play group, and finally move to the classroom.

Roleplays. Another analog tool for teaching social skill is the use of roleplays. These role-plays can be done with puppets or dolls, and are sometimes acted out by the child and an adult. The roleplay may either demonstrate the appropriate way to behave or may show an inappropriate behavior and call upon the child to correct the error. For example, we might show the child two puppets in conversation, but have one puppet fail to make eye contact with the second. We would ask the child what was wrong and ask him to fix the problem. In this example, he would need to turn the first puppet around so it faced the second puppet during the conversation.

Social Stories. Carol Gray's social stories have become a widely used tool for helping children with autism learn new social skills. Using this method, a teacher or parent identifies a social situation that is problematic for the child, and then writes a simple story describing the child dealing appropriately with the situation. The stories might be illustrated with photographs or line drawings of the child, or they might just consist of words on a page, depending on the child's age and reading abilities. Younger children may need illustrations to help them follow the words.

Table 1-4 has an example of a social story that we used with a boy who averted his gaze when interacting with others. Our social stories may differ slightly from Gray's suggestions, but are rooted in and inspired by her work in this area. In Chapter Three, we will describe in more detail how social stories may be useful in teaching children the rules that guide social behavior. You may also want to refer to *The Original Social Story Book* by Carol Gray.

Table 1-4 | Eye Contact in a Conversation

Talking to people is fun. I like to talk to people. When I talk to others, I look in their eyes. This is important to remember. I need to look when they are speaking to me so that they know I am listening. Looking at people makes them feel important and happy. It is also important to look when I am listening. That helps people know I am paying attention to them. Then they will know I am interested in what they are saying. People will be happy when I look at them. They will think I am a good friend. I can be a good friend. I can remember to look at others when we are talking together

---

Naturalistic Instruction

Incidental teaching, a kind of naturalistic instruction, is an ABA technique that takes advantage of a child's interest in events and items in the natural environment in order to teach. For example, if your child is surrounded by several toys and picks up a ball, you could focus your play and language teaching on ball play. This way you allow him to take the lead in selecting items of interest. Similarly, during your child's bath time you may talk about the soap and washcloth, and at dinner discuss the names of foods.

One of the strengths of incidental teaching is that it allows you to capitalize on naturally occurring events as teaching opportunities. Unlike discrete trial instruction, where you may have to make a special effort to help your child transfer the skill beyond the teaching situation, in incidental teaching he is learning the skill in the setting in which it will be used.

Keeping Data

One of the essentials of good ABA teaching is record keeping. This is because you need objective evidence that your child has mastered one skill before you move on to teaching the next skill. Every day you should spend at least a few minutes keeping track of how many correct responses your child makes to the questions you pose or requests you make, how long he plays, or how many prompts he needs to do a task. The specific data depend on the skill being taught. For example, if he is learning to manipulate toys, you might record the number of correct manipulations. If he is learning independent play, your record could reflect the number of minutes he played by himself. We expect a child to get at least 90 percent of his trials correct over 2 to 3 sessions before we move on to the next step of a program.

For more information on record keeping, see the books *Behavioral Intervention for Young Children with Autism: A Manual for Parents and Professionals* by Catherine Maurice et al., or *Steps to Independence* by Bruce Baker and Alan Brightman, listed in the References at the end of this chapter.

The Role of the Home Consultant

This book is written for adults working with a child in a home-based program or a center-based program located in a preschool or elementary school, or a public or private special education program. Many children may have a combination of these two types of programs, with home programming complementing a center-based program. Other children have a program that is run exclusively from the home.

Wherever your child goes to school, we assume that you have access to a "home behavioral consultant" who is familiar with your child's learning pattern and knows how to match teaching programs to your child's individual strengths and needs. A home consultant, or behavioral consultant, is an expert in applied behavior analysis who helps you design and implement teaching programs for use at home.

In this book, we often suggest that you ask your child's home consultant to help you develop new programs. (If your child is in a school-based program, then the behavioral consultant in the school fills that same role.) This book is not a satisfactory substitute for an expert who knows your child. The techniques of applied behavior analysis are complex and if you are doing this work alone, it may be difficult to make as much progress as you might wish.

We hope you will find someone with expertise to be your guide in working with your child. You may wish to consult our previous book, *Right from the Start* (Woodbine House, 1997), for information on finding services and on the role different professionals can play in your child's education. There is also a useful discussion of these issues in the book, *Behavioral Intervention for Young Children with Autism: A Manual for Parents and Professionals,* by Catherine Maurice and her colleagues (Pro-Ed, 1996).

A note of caution: We are concerned about the credentials of many of the individuals who are offering services as private consultants for families of children with autism. Although there are many superbly skilled practitioners, there are countless others whose training is limited and who have an inflated sense of their own expertise. It remains a "buyer beware" market. We are nonetheless heartened by the increasing awareness of these problems and by the movement toward national credentialing for people who wish to be recognized as having special expertise in applied behavior analysis. Consumers should look carefully at the background and training of individuals who offer private consulting services.

Ideally, a behavioral consultant should be a Board Certified Behavior Analyst. However, this certification process is a relatively recent one and not every capable behavioral consultant has completed the process of certification. For details on the credentials the Behavior Analyst Certification Board requires for an individual to be eligible to be board certified, you can check the website at www.bacb.com or write to BACB at 519 E. Park Ave., Tallahassee, FL 32301. This will give you a set of standards against which to judge people who present themselves as behavioral consultants or home consultants. At a minimum, you want someone who meets these credentials or works under the supervision of someone who does.

Who Can Benefit from These Instructional Programs?

Children with autism have a wide range of skills and abilities that will influence what they learn from the instructional programs described in this book. Some children will move through most of the programs with ease, while others, because they struggle with prerequisite skills, will never master all of the material we offer here. Parents and teachers have to judge what in this book is appropriate for their child and when.

In the Introduction, we explained that the methods in this book work best with children who are in preschool or elementary school and who have a diagnosis of Autistic Disorder, Asperger's Disorder, or Pervasive Developmental Disorder Not Otherwise Specified (Atypical Autism).

Some other factors that are important in deciding whether your child is ready for these programs include: your child's developmental level, his speech and language skills, his previous experience in learning through ABA methods, and his behavior.

Developmental Level. Some children on the spectrum of autism have mental retardation in addition to their autism, and they will move more slowly through these programs. There will also be limits to their ability to master the more complex material. However, it is often difficult to assess the learning po-

tential of a very young child with autism and the best way to find out if he can master a skill is to give him a good opportunity to learn it. Adaptations in teaching methods can be made as you find out how your child responds to a program. This feedback loop of teaching, evaluating your child's performance, and adapting the teaching methods allows you to tailor your teaching to your child in an increasingly precise fashion over time.

Speech and Language Skills. Children also vary in the speech and language skills and the social awareness they bring to this learning, and this will influence the speed with which they master new material. Children who have very good receptive language will typically make greater progress than those who do not. (By receptive language, we mean an individual's ability to understand what other people say to him.) However, many of the programs can be modified for children who have more limited language. For example, the use of photographs, drawings, or written words may help some children who have trouble understanding spoken language. For example, photographs might remind a child to follow a schedule of activities or go through all the steps of a routine. We will describe in later chapters situations where pictures or other visual cues can help children learn.

Previous ABA Experience. These programs should not be the first ABA teaching you do with your child. Before you begin the programs in this book, your child should have completed some basic instructional programs. For example, he should be able to comply with your directions and imitate simple gestures. In each chapter, we identify prerequisite skills your child needs before working on the material in that chapter.

Behavior. Any behavior problems your child exhibits should not be so frequent as to make other teaching difficult. The management of some serious behavior problems is a book in itself. For minor problems, sometimes simple solutions such as ignoring tantrums or briefly holding your child's hands on his lap if he hits are sufficient when combined with abundant rewards for good behavior. These are the same discipline methods any savvy parent uses with a young child.

When children with autism pose more difficult behavior problems, the solution may involve getting a "functional behavioral assessment." In this type of assessment, a behavioral consultant or teacher observes your child to determine what is motivating his behavior and what he may be trying to communicate through his behavior. (See, for example, *Severe Behavior Problems,* by V. Mark Durand.) Your child is then taught an alternative to misbehavior that can accomplish the same purpose. For example, a child who throws tantrums to get out of work can be taught to ask for a break from an activity.

Under the Individuals with Disabilities Education Act, public schools are required to provide a functional behavioral assessment for any student with an IEP whose behavior hinders learning. However, getting a school-provided assessment might not be the best option if the person who does the school's assessments is not experienced in working with students with autism. These functional assessments can be complex and are best done under the direction of someone who is familiar with applied behavior analysis methods used to control disruptive behavior. Your behavioral consultant will know how to do this kind of assessment.

Summary

When it follows a typical pattern, the social development of children appears to unfold in a relatively effortless fashion. Although they have to be taught the social rules of their culture, children everywhere enjoy the company of others. By contrast, children with autism do not seem to share this innate pleasure in the company of others. They must be taught to play, to reciprocate social approaches, to tell jokes, and the countless other behaviors that are part of the childhood social repertoire. This book introduces the reader to applied behavior analysis techniques for facilitating play, social skills, and perspective-taking by children with autism. We will also discuss skills that are most readily taught in a classroom with typically developing peers and how to prepare your child for such an experience.

References

Baker, B. L., Brightman, A. J., Blacher, J., & Heifetz, L. (1997). *Steps to independence: Teaching everyday skills to children with special needs.* Baltimore, MD: Paul H. Brookes.

Cox, R. (1993). Normal childhood development from birth to five years. In E. Schopler, M. E. Van Bourgondien, & M. Bristol (Eds.), *Preschool issues in autism* (pp. 39-57). New York: Plenum.

Durand, V. M. (1990). *Severe behavior problems. A Functional communication training approach.* New York: Guilford Press.

Gray, C. (1993). *The original social story book.* Arlington, TX: Future Horizons.

Harris, S. L. & Weiss, M. J. (1997). *Right from the start: Behavioral intervention for young children with autism.* Bethesda, MD: Woodbine House.

Maurice, C., Green, G. & Luce, S. C., Eds. (1996). *Behavioral intervention for young children with autism: A manual for parents and professionals.* Austin, TX: Pro-Ed.

2 | Teaching Play Skills

In the beginning, it seemed far removed from real play. When Jack and Allison began teaching Scott to play with them, Jack would sit cross-legged on the floor. Scott would be nearby, but turned away and paying no attention to his father. Jack would reach over and touch Scott on the shoulder saying, "OK, Scott, let's play ball." Scott would turn to look at his dad, who would ruffle his son's hair, saying, "Good boy, let's play." Then, Jack would spread his legs in a v-shape and when Scott did not follow suit, he would tap the boy's foot. Scott would look at his dad and spread his own legs.

In the alley formed by their outspread legs, Jack rolled the ball to his son. Scott might touch the ball and push it slightly toward his father. Jack would then reach over, pat Scott's arm, give him a bit of cookie, and say, "Great playing ball." They would roll the ball three or four times, and when they stopped, Jack would toss Scott in the air, saying "Way to go, little guy."

That was the first step. When Scott responded consistently to his father's invitation to play ball, Jack made the activity a little more challenging by moving away from Scott when they played. Over a few weeks, Jack moved a few inches farther with each session, and Scott continued to roll the ball to him. When they were four feet apart, Jack made another change in the routine. He invited his five-year-old daughter, Rita, to play with them.

For the first session with Rita, Jack positioned the three of them about four feet from one another. He rolled the ball to Scott and let him roll it back, and then he rolled the ball to Rita and let her roll it back to him. Scott seemed very comfortable with this arrangement, so Jack moved on to the next step, in which Rita and

Scott played with one another. For this play session, Jack sat with his legs folded behind Rita and Rita sat opposite Scott. Before they started, Jack reminded Rita to "get really happy" if Scott pushed the ball to her. Rita looked at her brother, called, "Let's play ball" and rolled the ball to him. Scott looked a bit puzzled, but saw his father sitting behind Rita and pushed the ball in their direction. Rita, remembering her father's advice, yelled, "Way to go, Scotty!"

After another session in which Jack sat behind Rita, he began to edge farther back until he was sitting several feet behind her. Next he began gradually moving to the side. After a couple of weeks, he was standing in the doorway while the children rolled the ball back and forth. All the while, Rita shouted words of encouragement to her little brother. It was the first time she had ever really played with Scott and it was thrilling to have him as a playmate.

Once that first game was established, Rita was eager to do more and Scott seemed accepting of the play sessions. Allison and Jack decided to build on their success. Their next step was to exchange a truck for the ball and the words, "Let's play trucks" for the former "Let's play ball." This change went smoothly and encouraged them to find other things the children could do together.

How Does the Kimballs' Experience Resemble Your Own?

As we mentioned in Chapter One, it is important for a child with autism to master some basic play skills before playing with other children. Jack and Allison Kimball recognized this and worked with Matt Becker, their home consultant, to teach Scott these skills. Laying the groundwork for a single game took several weeks and some skillful teaching on Jack's part.

Once Scott mastered rolling the ball to his father, it was relatively easy to introduce his sister, Rita, as a playmate. This not only enabled Scott and Rita to play together, it also helped Jack and Allison learn about effective teaching methods. They began to appreciate that they could use the same approach they had used to teach Scott other skills, such as pointing to pictures and imitating sounds, to help him learn to play. They saw that applied behavior analysis (ABA) was more than discrete trial teaching. It could be used creatively to teach Scott a range of social and play skills. The foundation of

this learning involved many tiny steps in discrete trial format, but over time Scott moved toward true childhood play.

Once they were hooked on using ABA to teach Scott how to play and enjoy other children's company, the Kimballs added more programs. They introduced him to other toys, including toy animals, trucks, and crayons. Soon they started working on basic pretend play skills, encouraging him to roll a car and feed a doll. After Scott could play with a range of toys and had pretend play skills, the Kimballs incorporated Rita into the games and then increased the complexity of the play between the children.

Whether your child needs to start with basic toy manipulation programs like Scott, or can move directly to more complex programs involving another child, you should find material in this chapter to increase your child's play skills.

A good beginning for teaching your child to play with other children is to first teach her to play with you. In that situation she can master the techniques of manipulating the toys, receive a great deal of reinforcement for her efforts, and have a partner who is always alert to her needs. Play with adults is a good place to begin.

If there is another young child in your family, she may be a ready-made playmate. However, it is important to respect the needs of your typically developing child. Be certain she wants to play with her sibling with autism and do not ask her to spend more than a few minutes each day in the play programs. Jack and Allison kept Rita's role modest and asked her to join Scott only when they knew he was in a good mood and ready to play. They wanted Rita to enjoy these sessions and gave her abundant praise. They never forced her to play and always let her know how much they appreciated her help.

If you do not have another child, or if your own child is reluctant to join in these games, you can ask other children in the neighborhood, a young relative, or children of people at your place of worship to help. School teachers, neighbors, scout leaders, and Sunday school teachers may also be able to suggest peers who would be willing playmates. Initially, it should be sufficient to have one or two children who each come once a week for half an hour. Later you can expand the circle of children who are playmates. You can make these sessions fun for the children and also make them rewarding with a special treat after the play session.

If your child has serious behavior problems, you will need to address these before you focus on social skills. Find an expert in applied behavior analysis (a teacher, psychologist, or an ABA certified consultant) who can work with you to design a program. If your child is more behaviorally challenged or has more mental retardation than Scott, you will need to go more slowly with the programs, but much of what we are addressing is relevant for children with significant impairments as well as for those with milder symptoms. Systematic teaching can help even slow learners master many skills.

In the pages that follow, we first discuss how children typically learn to play and how this process goes awry for children who have autism. We then describe teaching programs for children at different skill levels. Select programs that meet your child's needs, but do be certain that your son or daughter has the prerequisite skills for more advanced programs before you begin.

How Do Kids Learn to Play?

The development of play, like the development of motor abilities or language, unfolds over time. Play grows more social, more imaginative, and more complex as children get older. As shown in Table 2-1, there is a predictable progression of play-related behaviors.

Table 2-1	The Development of Play	
Play-Related Skill	**Age**
Shakes rattle	7 Months
Reaches for out-of-reach toy	8 Months
Waves bye-bye	10 Months
Shows toy	15 Months
Pulls toy	18 Months
Parallel play	24 Months
Helps put away toys	30 Months
Associative play (some sharing)	42 Months
Cooperates with other children	48 Months
Builds building with blocks	48 Months
Dresses up in adult clothes	60 Months

Play has roots in early development. The four-month-old looks at a rattle placed in her hand and begins to bring it to her mouth, although she may drop it before she gets it all the way to her face. By seven months, she will grasp the rattle with one hand and shake it. At this age, she chews on toys and reaches toward objects that interest her. The shaking of a rattle or pushing of a ball gradually develops into interactive play with a parent. At ten months, not only is she getting better at picking things up and holding onto them, she is also playing social games. She waves bye-bye and can participate in "pat-a-cake." By eleven months, she sits alone well and her hands are free to manipulate objects. She will offer an item to another person, but does not always have the ability to release it from her grasp.

If you laugh at something a one-year-old does, she will be delighted and do it again. She has learned simple imitative games to play with adults and enjoys doing them many times over. A few months later, walking freely and fully mobile, the child of fifteen months is busy exploring, tugging, carrying, and giving. At eighteen months, she will pull a toy behind her.

By two years of age, the child is running, kicking a ball, building a tower of blocks, and pretending to feed her doll. During their second year, children incorporate more and more pretending into their play. What begins with feeding a stuffed animal becomes more elaborate over time. Although the two-year-old is not yet capable of interactive play with other children, she enjoys being around them. If she sees a toy another child has, she may grab it, and get into trouble with the other youngster who is not ready to share.

The child's ability to interact with other children will improve a great deal when she is three years old. Three-year-olds can share, wait their turn, and cooperate with another child in play. From this age forward, play grows increasingly interpersonal and complex. Older children spend much of their time in fantasy play and can weave a story line together, elaborating on their play and varying the outcome as it pleases them. In these games they can be anything they wish to be—firefighter, veterinarian, teacher, daddy, or mommy.

Levels of Socialization in Play

Before they can play together, children show an interest in one another. Even babies show a special interest in other children. Well before they can walk, talk, or share toys, children will show, by the direction of their gaze, a clear awareness of other small people around them. Around one year of age, children may exchange a toy with a familiar peer (Cox, 1993). During the second year, these pleasurable interactions, as well as aggressive behaviors, increase as children learn how to play with one another.

Table 2-2 | Levels of Socialization in Play

Solitary Play—Child plays by self.

Parallel Play—Child plays near another child, may show interest or occasionally exchange toys, but not really interactive.

Associative Play—Several children are engaged in the same play and interact with one another. They share equipment or toys, but each child goes her own way.

Cooperative Play—Children work together toward common goal or share a fantasy theme that requires mutual exchange to build scenario.

There are four different levels of socialization in play. As illustrated in Table 2-2, play initially tends to be solitary, with the child manipulating objects on her own. For very young children, playing together essentially means sitting next to each other with minimal interaction except for the occasional exchange of items. Gradually, this parallel play gives way to a more interactive format called associative play in which children share objects and may be part of the same game, but each plays in her own way. For example, two children might both build with blocks or color a mural, but not work together on the same creation. Finally, in cooperative play, children collaborate to create a mutual project or share a fantasy scenario. This might include pretending to be a teacher and student or a doctor and a patient with a shared story line between the youngsters.

How Do Kids with Autism Learn to Play?

Play skills in children with autism do not follow the same trajectory as they do in typically developing children. Differences include:

- a tendency to play with toys in repetitive ways,
- problems in learning through observation,
- seemingly immature play skills,
- limited or no pretend play.

Repetitive Play with Toys. The way children with autism manipulate toys is often highly repetitive and rote. For example, a child might stack blocks in the same order, red-blue-yellow, knock them down, say "whoops," and then build them up again. Another child might bring a toy up close to her eyes, turn it repeatedly, but never use it for its intended purpose. Many children with autism enjoy toys for their sensory qualities, instead of for their intended function. For example, Scott Kimball lined up toy cars to enjoy the pattern they created instead of using them as toy cars. Another child might sit in the sandbox and push her fingers through the sand for the sensation on her fingers, rather than to do anything creative with the sand.

Difficulties Learning through Observation. Difficulties in learning by watching others also influence play-related behavior in children with autism. Unlike other children, who learn to use a toy by watching a child or adult play with it, the child with autism often does not attend to how others manipulate objects. Even when her parents deliberately show her how to push a truck or feed a doll, she will simply ignore that model. This cuts her off from an important channel of learning to play.

Immature Play. Another distinctive feature of the play of children with autism is that it is developmentally immature. The young child with autism may simply mouth toys or bang them together at an age when other children are playing with toys as they are intended to be used. Some children with autism may enjoy solitary play with blocks and puzzles, as well as looking at books.

However, their use of these items is often rote and repetitive in contrast to the creative variation of other children. The social elements of creative play seen in typically developing children are usually absent. That is, they do not make up elaborate and continually changing story lines to go with their toy manipulation.

As a result of these factors, the play of children with autism is immature in relation to their developmental age. This is a problem because play skills and social skills build on one another. If your child does not learn to manipulate toys, she will have a hard time using them to interact with another child.

Difficulties with Pretend Play. Although many children with autism engage in no pretend play, we know some youngsters who show the early stages of pretend play. They may feed a doll or bring plastic food for a parent to pretend to eat. However, these fantasies are limited to a few "scripts" and do not show the rich variation of their peers' pretend play. Some children with autism will passively cooperate with the fantasy play of older siblings. For example, a young child with autism might be assigned the role of "baby" in the family and then be left to play quietly or respond in a structured way to an older sister's instructions. She does not, however, take part in building the fantasy, as a child without autism would.

Why Do Differences in Play Skills Matter?

Almost every family we have worked with has identified play as a high priority for their young child. That is a very appropriate goal because play is one of the primary activities of childhood and one of the key ways in which young children interact with one another.

If a child's play has an immature or odd quality, it sets her apart from other children. So, too, does the inability to reciprocate another child's invitation to play. Such differences in play can make children with autism seem unappealing as potential playmates and friends. Furthermore, a child who cannot play with other children will miss one of the most important ways in which young children relate to one another and will be denied the opportunity to develop a whole range of other social skills, such as learning to cooperate with other children, to empathize with their concerns, and to work collaboratively to develop ideas.

Play skills should be a focus of instruction throughout your child's ABA program. Just as in teaching communication or cognitive skills, there should be a continual focus on increasing the complexity of play and expanding the themes of your child's play.

As you begin to teach play skills, it is helpful to remember that these skills will be built slowly and systematically. One skill lays the groundwork for the next. Taking it slowly requires considerable patience and time, and some of the early steps may seem remote from the spontaneous play of childhood. However, this gradual approach maximizes the likelihood that your child will reach that long-term goal.

Building Blocks of Play

Regardless of your child's current play behaviors, you can help her develop more play skills. In this section, we describe how to teach toy manipulation, parallel play, sharing an activity, sustained independent play, and pretend play. We also describe Playbooks and Play Stations as tools for teaching.

Most children with autism have sufficient fine and gross motor skills to do these programs. However, if your child has significant motor impairments, she may well need some physical therapy services. The PT can not only support her learning, but also adapt the materials being used, if needed. For example, small balls could be replaced with large ones.

Although the programs in this chapter begin with basic skills, there are some things your child needs to know before you start a program. We call these "prerequisites" and they are described in each section. For example, one prerequisite for toy manipulation is the ability to follow adult directions such as "come here" or "sit down." Your child should also be able to sit for a brief period of time and respond to your requests and directions. If your child cannot sit still and follow simple directions, you should teach these skills before anything else. A discussion of these kinds of basic instructional skills can be found in our book *Right from the Start: Behavioral Intervention for Young Children with Autism* (Woodbine House, 1998).

Toy Manipulation

The goal, or first target of instruction for play, is imitating actions with toys. In these programs, your child learns to do the things you do. In later programs, she learns to do what other children do. But first she must imitate you. For example, she learns to roll a car, hold a play phone next to her ear, or put a ring on a stacker.

These early programs are improving your child's ability to "watch and do," which will be essential for more complex play. These programs also introduce your child to the functions of objects, providing the opportunity to use toys as they are intended, rather than in the stereotyped ways that are typical of children with autism. This ability to imitate helps build a repertoire of appropriate actions with play materials.

As discussed in Chapter One, you should keep data about your child's progress in learning these skills. Note the number of correct manipulations per opportunities given. For example, if you offer your child 6 opportunities and she gets 4 correct, her percentage correct would be 67 percent. We usually look for 90 percent correct over 2 or 3 consecutive days or sessions before we increase the complexity of a program.

One-Step Toy Manipulations

If your child needs to start at square one in imitating actions with toys, you should start with one-step, or single action, toy manipulations. Initially, one-step toy manipulations that are taught through nonverbal imitation focus on the most important, common actions with that object. For example, you could teach your child to roll a car, to place a peg in a hole, or to put a shape in a sorter box. Doing this involves modeling an action and asking your child to do the same. For example, you might say to your child, "Do this" and roll a car.

It is important that you do not stop with teaching your child one action per toy. After she has learned five or six basic one-step toy imitations, you want to teach her to imitate any action with the play object. Otherwise, she may memorize a single action for a particular object and become rigid in her use of the item. In that case, she might be responding to the presence of the object (for example, the toy car) instead of watching what you do. Limiting the use of an object to a single action could seriously impair your child's ability to learn to play. For this reason, it is important that you teach more than one action for each object. You might teach your child to roll a car, put a doll in the car, and put the car in the garage. This way, you are building a flexible repertoire of play skills. You are also ensuring that she develops the ability to observe and imitate the actions of another person. That "watch and do" will pay off in a big way later.

Two-Step Toy Manipulations

After your child develops one-step toy manipulations, you will work on two-step toy manipulation skills which require your child to perform a sequence of two actions. This will help your child learn to attend to a sequence of actions with play materials such as opening a barn door and taking out the cow. Table 2-3 shows items that lend themselves to this kind of sequencing.

Again, it is important to introduce variability with the play materials so your child will not develop only a narrow range of play abilities. It is also important to ensure that she continues to imitate you and not do things in a rote way when she sees a toy. For this reason, once a child has learned a few basic sequences, we usually start teaching unrelated play sequences as well as related ones. For example, your child might imitate your rolling a car and then putting a ring on a stacker or putting a doll in a car and putting a cow in the barn. These play chains (sequences) may not only be unrelated, but even illogical. For example, you

Table 2-3 | Activities for Two-Step Toy Manipulation

Logical:

- Put doll in car/roll car
- Put car in barn/close barn door
- Open toy purse/take out comb
- Scribble with crayon/put crayon in box
- Put doll in airplane/move airplane in air

Illogical:

- Put comb in car/roll car
- Put crayon in bucket/put doll in cup
- Put stacker ring in barn/Put cow in play purse
- Roll doll like car/put doll in barn
- Put cow in airplane/put airplane in play purse

might put the cow in a car and the stacker ring in a bucket. The critical element in these chains is imitation. Expanding these skills into illogical and unrelated chains ensures that your child's imitative skills are firmly established. Be a little unpredictable!

Parallel Play

Parallel play marks the beginnings of social play in childhood. In parallel play, two children sit near each other and play with similar objects, but do not yet truly interact. For example, each may play with blocks or scribble on paper. Learning to engage in parallel play teaches your child to tolerate sharing space with another child, gives you opportunities to build longer play sequences, and lays the groundwork for your child to imitate peers in the classroom.

One prerequisite for parallel play is the ability to work independently at an activity such as coloring, building with blocks, rolling cars, or stacking rings. After your child has learned a couple of these activities and can start and stop them appropriately, you can use them as the first activities of parallel play.

Parallel Play with a Parent

You are your child's first playmate for parallel play. Sit next to her in a comfortable spot. The floor is a good choice because so much play goes on there. You can use a small table if you prefer. Have two sets of play materials, one for you and one for your child. Begin to play with your own materials. For example, pick up a crayon and start to color. If your child does not join in coloring with her own materials, prompt her to do so. Whenever possible, avoid verbal prompts such as "pick up the crayon," or "put it there." Instead, use gestures or physical prompts from behind her. Children tend to become dependent on verbal prompts and they are harder to fade (reduce) than gestures or support from behind.

When your child starts coloring, reinforce her effort with praise and tangible rewards, if needed. Keep reinforcing her as she continues her play and you continue yours. (Refer back to Chapter One for information on reinforcement.) Gradually increase the amount of time she plays next to you.

Parallel Play with Another Child

When your child can play independently in proximity to you for at least six or seven minutes, you can introduce another child. This helps her use her skills in a more typical context. Initially, you should give the children two different sets of materials, for example, crayons for your child and a stacker ring for the other youngster. Give each child a toy that she likes. Later, you will use identical materials to lay the groundwork for more interactive play.

If there are toys that hold a particular fascination for your child and she tends to play with them in a rigid fashion, do not use these toys for teaching at this stage. Later, when she has become more flexible, you can reinforce her for using these toys in novel ways.

Many children with autism will ignore another child unless that youngster intrudes on them. Initially, you may want your child simply to tolerate physical proximity to another child. If having another youngster close by is upsetting, separate them by a greater distance and gradually move them closer. You can also continue to reward your child for tolerating the presence of the other child. At this stage of instruction, however, it is best if she can accept delays in getting these rewards or can respond to subtle incentives such as smiles, pats, or putting a token in a cup where she can see it. Otherwise, giv-

ing her rewards may disrupt the flow of play with her peer.

In selecting a child to act as a peer for these parallel play sessions, look for someone who is cooperative, has appropriate play skills, and seems like a good model of parallel play. Remember that you may be a more rewarding presence for the peer than your own child can be, and be sure to lavish praise on both children. A treat after play is always a good idea. Try to be sure the peer leaves feeling that she wants to come back again.

Video Modeling

If your child enjoys videos, you have available a potent tool for teaching play skills. There are a number of advantages to using videos for teaching. One is that you can show a skill being used in different settings and lay the foundation for generalization of the skill. Another advantage is that the person on the tape becomes the model for appropriate behavior and you can focus your attention on prompting your child to respond rather than being both model and prompter. Learning to do what a child on videotape does is a good way to help your child become more skilled in learning by watching others.

Although you could use a tape of an adult, a child model is preferable because you want your child to learn to imitate other children. The tape can be of a family member or another familiar child so that your child also has access to that peer as a live model.

Table 2-4 | Prerequisites for Using Video Modeling

1. Do one-step imitation with toys
2. Attend from at least a five-foot distance
3. Show an interest in videotapes

Table 2-4 shows that before you introduce your child to videotape modeling, she should be able to do one-step imitation with toys when she watches you. For example, she should be able to put a block in a cup or put a peg in a board. She should also be able to attend to something happening five feet away from her and she should have an interest in videotapes. If she can do all of these things, you can try videotapes as a teaching tool.

To begin a video modeling session, seat your child facing the TV monitor with the appropriate play materials in front of her. Make sure the videotape is at the right spot so that when you push the button the information you want will be played without distraction. Push the play button and say to her, "Do this." She should then watch the video clip and copy the action with her own materials. If she imitates correctly, you should reward her. If her response is incorrect, rewind the tape and repeat the trial. Keep a record of her performance by dividing the total number she got correct by the total number of trials. For example, if she had 7 trials and got 6 correct, her percentage correct would be 86 percent.

The best way to approach this instruction is to begin with one-step imitation and build up to two and three steps. You can directly reinforce your child or have the reinforcement built into the videotape. For example, you could show a brief clip of a program your child enjoys as a reward, or there could be an instruction on the tape to take a break.

Be sure that the videotape shows a close-up of the action you want your child to imitate and leave about five seconds between trials on the tape. You may want to put ten or fifteen trials on a tape so you don't have to keep rewinding it. If the purpose is to teach your child to imitate a single video-modeled skill, you might tape many repetitions of one action. Otherwise, you can tape several different actions so she has to attend closely to the tape to recognize exactly what she is supposed to do.

Sometimes it takes flexibility and "tinkering" to find just the right way to teach a child a new skill. As shown in the box on the next page, that was the situation with Jenny. An advanced form of video modeling enabled us to teach her social skills we had not been able to teach with other strategies. This kind of problem solving by teachers, parents, and their ABA consultants can often make the difference between a child who grows increasingly frustrated with a lesson she cannot learn and one who moves forward gracefully. When a child who has shown the capacity to learn other skills gets "stuck," it is important to try alternatives. You may need the help of an ABA consultant to decide which alternatives are most appropriate.

Sharing an Activity

Once your child masters parallel play, she is ready to learn to play cooperatively. The first steps in cooperative play are sharing materials and taking turns. In order to learn to share an activity, your child will need the prerequisite skills of completing an activity on her own and being able to sustain at least a few minutes of parallel play. When your child learns to share an activity, she will learn to tolerate sharing materials, develop cooperative play skills, and begin to interact with her peers.

Jennifer Learns to Play with Her Friends

Jennifer had a very hard time learning to play with her friends. Although the techniques we describe in this chapter had enabled her to master many early play skills, such as imitation of multi-step actions and basic pretend skills, when it came to using these skills with a friend she just "fell apart." She would ignore the other child and spend her time absorbed in repetitive behaviors. It was clear that Jennifer needed more help in learning to use her play repertoire in a social setting.

We decided to use video modeling to teach her more complex interactive, scripted play. Jenny and her classmate, David, who also had autism, would watch a brief, ninety-second videotape of two adults engaged in a pretend play sequence. On the videotape, the adult models played together at the kitchen area, setting the table for lunch, getting lunch ready, and sitting down to eat together.

In the beginning stages, Jenny and David needed help re-creating the scene and the teacher prompted them to engage in the script. Jenny even needed the words for her parts to be written on cards as a "script" for her to read aloud.

After a while, Jenny and David got very good at the lunch script. We then introduced variations on this theme by showing different scenarios on the videotape and encouraging Jenny and David to act them out. Among the variations were such things as making grilled cheese instead of tuna fish for lunch and cleaning up after lunch. The length of the videotape segments was also increased.

Eventually, no videotape was needed. Jenny and David could play at the kitchen area for five minutes, with no help from classroom staff. The variety of themes was extensive. Among the many scenarios they practiced were grocery store shopping, making a cake, taking a car ride, packing for vacation, and playing with a dollhouse.

Each time a new theme was introduced, a videotape was used initially to teach the concepts, themes, and actions central to that particular play activity. The stories for the new themes were short in duration to help build success. The children often needed nonverbal prompts to facilitate skill acquisition. Jenny, for example, really needed those written scripts in front of her. Ultimately, the use of written scripts and even the observation of the videotapes were faded. The children played in varied ways across many different activity centers.

Ball Play

In the beginning of this chapter, Scott's parents chose ball play as their first shared activity. Ball play is an excellent example of how skills build on one another and can be used to teach sharing. The very nature of ball play requires frequent exchanges, and the rhythm of the game gives the child many opportunities to receive the ball and to pass it on. Mastery of simple ball play prepares your child for more interactive skills and for ball play that demands more language. Learning this skill increases your child's capacity to imitate appropriate play behaviors, builds her sustained attention, gives her eye-hand and gross motor

practice, and prepares her for other sports games that children play in school and in the community. Table 2-5 lists the various stages of ball play discussed in this chapter.

Table 2-5 | The Stages of Ball Play

1. Imitate ball manipulation
2. Follow receptive commands for ball manipulation
3. Engage in reciprocal ball play
4. Practice basic sports skills (e.g., bounce and throw a basketball)

To learn ball play, your child should have well-established compliance skills (Table 2-6). She should follow your directions most of the time (about 90 percent) without much fuss. She should be able to manipulate fifteen to twenty-five different objects and imitate at least five to ten of your one-step actions with the instruction to "Do this." For example, she should be able to imitate you in raising her arms, turning around, stamping her feet, and dropping a block in a box.

Table 2-6 | Prerequisites for Ball Play Imitation

1. Demonstrate general compliance with your commands
2. Imitate 15 to 25 one-step toy manipulations
3. Imitate 5 to 10 nonverbal one-step play gestures

Basic Ball Play. To teach basic imitative ball play, sit facing your child in a chair or on the floor. Choose a ball big enough that she can comfortably handle it. You will eventually want to use several different sizes and colors of balls so she generalizes her skill to different balls. To start the session, give her the instruction "Do this" and perform an action with the ball such as transferring it from one hand to the other. Then hand her the ball. Teach her several different ways of manipulating the ball, including throwing, kicking, and rolling.

Ball Play with Receptive Commands. After she learns to imitate your handling of the ball, you will teach your child to follow receptive commands with the ball. The prerequisites for this program include imitating what you do with a ball and following directions with toys. To teach receptive commands for ball play, sit on the floor or stand facing your child. Give a direction such as "Throw me the ball" or "Kick the ball." The most common commands are to bounce, roll, kick, throw, or catch the ball.

If your child does not have the necessary receptive language, you can initially prompt her by having a second adult stand behind her and guide her in throwing or kicking in response to your command. Picture cues of how to throw or kick may also help some children. You want her to follow your command and not simply imitate you, so it is better to have the other person provide the prompts rather than do it yourself.

Reciprocal Ball Play. The next step, reciprocal ball play, is your road to interactive play and again offers the opportunity to increase the duration of sustained play. Your child should be reliably imitating (at least 90 percent of the time) what you do with objects before you teach her this reciprocal exchange (Table 2-7). She should also be able to follow a couple of commands in a row before you need to offer a reward. Reciprocal ball play is a skill that can be taught in a small group, and, very importantly, it offers opportunities for other children in your family to become play partners (as Rita did with her brother, Scott).

Table 2-7 | Prerequisites for Reciprocal Ball Play

1. Demonstrate general compliance with your commands
2. Have mastered ball play imitation
3. Have mastered ball play receptive commands

The basic objective of this program is teaching your child to reciprocate your ball play gestures. For example, you roll it to her and she rolls it to you, or you kick it to her and she kicks it back. As you act out this sequence, you can give some minimal reinforcers (e.g., "Good throw") along the way. You should, however, save your most powerful reinforcers (e.g., juice) as a reward for completing a specified number of exchanges. Initially this might be a single exchange, but eventually your child should be able to complete numerous exchanges prior to earning a major reward. When she can sustain ten to fifteen exchanges with no reinforcement until the end of the play sequence, she is ready to play with a peer. Your child may need help remembering where to sit or stand during the exchange and you might put a carpet square on the floor or use tape to mark off her space.

Basic Sport Skills. The final step in Table 2-5 is to practice basic sports skills. Ball play lends itself to many variations on the basic theme. These variations teach your child to use sports equipment and prepare her for the group games that she will encounter in school and in the community. Some children take months, others a few weeks, to acquire these skills. The length of time will vary, but if these skills are taught systematically, many children can learn to shoot baskets or kick a soccer ball in some form of modified competition.

Acquiring sports skills gives your child good ways to play with her siblings. She may find that there is fun in sports, and the games may become inherently enjoyable for her. For example, once she can throw and bounce a ball, she can learn to play basketball. You will need a basketball net set at a proper level for her height and a large ball that she can handle comfortably. The first step is to have her imitate your throwing the ball into the net. You stand with her in front of the basket with the ball in your hands and say, "Let's play basketball." Then you shoot a basket and hand the ball to her. If she does not attempt to make a shot, give her a gestural prompt, pointing from the ball to the basket and then praise her effort. Be sure the net is set so that she can easily make a basket and gradually raise the height until it is a little challenging for her. You could also teach her to bounce the ball with one hand and then add some dribbling to the throwing pattern.

You want your child to have increasing numbers of exchanges of basket throws. You would start with one or two throws by each of you and gradually work up to four or five turns each before giving your child a reinforcer. Once she can take six or seven turns without a reinforcer, you might introduce a peer or a sibling into the game and let the children take turns shooting baskets. Moving around the court, passing, and dribbling can be added over time.

This type of instructional sequencing can be applied to any sport activity. Whatever the sport, remember to teach the components of the sequence separately prior to combining them in sequences. Also be sure to include variability in the sequences. This is important because real games will be random and unpredictable. For example, sometimes your child might start with the ball at one end of the court, sometimes the other, and sometimes she might shoot from the foul line and sometimes from under the basket. You must prepare your child for the different circumstances she is likely to encounter in the context of play.

Play Stations

"Play Stations" are activity centers set up at different physical locations scattered about a classroom. For example, you might have an art center with paper, crayons, and marking pens. Another center might have blocks of various sizes and colors, while a third station would consist of toy animals and a barn. This is a common arrangement in preschool and kindergarten classes and it is important for children with autism to learn to maneuver among these stations as preparation for a typical educational setting.

You can teach your child a number of skills with these centers. They can be used to increase her parallel play skills, to increase her ability to transfer imitation skills to a setting that resembles the typical preschool, and to help her tolerate transitions from one activity to another.

As shown in Table 2-8 on the next page, before your child is ready to use Play Stations she needs to follow your instructions, wait for reinforcement until the end of an activity, and have parallel play skills. She should be capable of at least four-step play imitations. For example, she should be able to copy another child who: 1) takes a toy car from the bin, 2) gets a doll from another bin, 3) puts the doll in the car, and 4) rolls the car to the garage.

Table 2-8 | Prerequisites for Using Play Stations

Before your child learns to use play stations she should:
1. Demonstrate general compliance with your commands
2. Have well established play imitation of at least four steps
3. Tolerate waiting for reinforcement
4. Have mastered parallel play skills

To teach your child to use Play Stations, set up several activity centers in different parts of the room. Initially, you may want to set up two centers. However, you should expand to at least four stations as soon as possible.

In setting up Play Stations, look for items that encourage children to play together as well as independently. Choose activities in which children must share materials, rather than more solitary activities such as computer games. Even when children are not actively collaborating, they should be sharing materials. For example, they might have to share crayons, paints, or other items in order to do the task. Choose activities that your child can do, but are not her absolute favorites. This will make it easier for her to share the materials. Later she can learn to tolerate sharing more attractive items, but initially you should make the sharing less difficult. Similarly, in the beginning you should make sure there are no other attractive toys or other activities to draw your child's attention away from the play stations. Later she needs to learn to ignore these other items.

Some examples of Play Station activities are listed in Table 2-9.

As in previous programs, you will be your child's first playmate and then you will invite her peers to be part of the play. And

**Table 2-9	Some Play Station Themes**		
◆ Puzzles	◆ Puppets	◆ Kitchen set
◆ Barnyard set	◆ Racecar track	◆ Train set
◆ Dolls	◆ Arts and crafts	◆ Blocks
◆ Construction toys		

as usual, you should start with short sessions and gradually increase the time.

To begin, say, "Let's play," walk to one center and begin to play with the materials. Remain with the task either for a set period of time or (depending on the task) until you have completed the activity. Then, you should walk to the next station. If your child does not follow you, give her a minimal physical or gestural prompt, but do not say anything. If a second person is helping you, just walk to the next station while the other adult provides a minimal physical or manual prompt, if needed. The reason for not saying something like "Come here" or "Go over there" is that you want to teach your child to follow other children and do what they do in the classroom. Continue this sequence for all four stations.

Start the sequence with activities your child likes least and end on the one she likes the most because this will make it easier for her to transition from one station to the next.

Be sure to vary the order of the stations each day so that your child learns to expect variety, not constancy. Depending on your child's skill level, you might begin with a single station and gradually build up to four to ten stations.

After your child can transition to four or five stations, it is time to introduce another child in place of the adult with whom she has been playing. If your child has a tantrum or resists playing with another child, you should be sure the activity is an appealing one, but does not require her to share her most favorite items. Keep the sessions brief. Also, be sure your child is well rested and in good humor when you start. You should have a plan for dealing with tantrums, such as a very brief "time out" during which she must sit and watch the other child play.

Sustained Independent Play

Typically developing children play with other people and also play on their own for extended periods. Although independent play is not a "social" skill in the sense that two or more children are interacting, the play skills developed are often useful for social as well as for solitary play. Skills developed in independent play, such as working puzzles or coloring, can transfer to social play. Independent play also helps your child fit into group settings. Children who cannot use toys appropriately look very different from their peers and this difference can be stigmatizing.

One of the bonuses of sustained independent play for parents is that the more your child plays alone, the more time you will have for other things. In other words, you may be able to turn your attention away from your child if you know she will be engaged in constructive activities.

The prerequisites for sustained independent play are listed in Table 2-10. To learn this skill your child has to be able to complete tasks that have a clear beginning and end such as assembling a puzzle, putting the pegs in a board, or playing a computer game. She also needs to sustain attention to these tasks without continual prompting and wait until the task is done before she is reinforced.

In addition, if your child engages in conspicuous self-stimulatory behavior while playing, you will need to bring that behavior under control before pursuing independent play. Stereotypic behavior makes a child look unusual to other youngsters and can be quite stigmatizing. It also interferes with a child's attention to a task and will reduce the amount of time she spends in play. Occasional self-stimulation can be addressed through redirection such as "put the pegs in the holes" or "take another crayon." If your child has more frequent self-stimulatory behavior, she will require a systematic ABA program to reduce the behavior. Such a program can be developed by your behavioral consultant based on a functional assessment of the behavior.

Table 2-10 | Prerequisites for Sustained Independent Play

1. Be able to complete play activities that have a clear beginning and end
2. Sustain attention to a task
3. Tolerate waiting for reinforcement

To encourage independent play, begin a teaching session by saying, "Play with the puzzles," or by having your child use a picture cue to direct herself to play. For example, she might follow a photographic activity schedule, as we discuss below in the section on Playbooks. Your child's task is to go to the toy and play with it for the amount of time you have selected as your initial goal. This will be brief in the early stages and gradually increase as she tolerates more independence.

Because you want your child to initiate and sustain this play on her own, keep verbal prompts to a minimum. Instead, use gestures and physical prompts while you stand behind her. Many children with autism become "prompt dependent" and it is better to keep words to a minimum and stay out of the picture as much as possible. If she does not seek reinforcement from you, but continues to play, that suggests the play itself has become rewarding. You will still want to reinforce her fine, independent play from time to time as you might praise any child for good behavior.

You should teach your child to use a variety of toys and activities so that she can move from one activity to the next and keep herself entertained for a long period. Keep records of how long she plays and how many prompts you used to keep her on task. Those records will help you decide if she is making progress toward independence.

Remember to start with brief periods and gradually build your child's tolerance for independent play. You might begin with a minute or two of play followed by a reinforcer and gradually build to three- to five-minute chunks of time. Separate play activities can then be chained together so that your child does a puzzle, gets her sorter box and plays with it, and then feeds her doll. After all three of those tasks, she might come to you and ask for juice as her reinforcement.

Playbooks

An effective way to help children chain several activities together is by using a series of photographs of the events. For example, your child might have a small loose-leaf notebook that has photos of a puzzle, a sorter box, and her doll, with the fourth picture being a cup of juice. These photos intended to help her stay on task are called Playbooks.

A Playbook is a photographic activity schedule (McClannahan & Krantz, 1999) designed to help a child develop a sequence of independent play activities. These books consist of a sequence of

pictures or words describing the activities the child should follow, with reinforcement periods built in. Your child is ready for a Playbook once she learns at least five different independent play activities such as coloring, playing with blocks, and doing a computer game, can wait until an activity is done for reinforcement, understands that pictures represent objects, and has the necessary fine motor and attending skills to seek out and pick up the items needed for play (Table 2-11).

Table 2-11 | Prerequisites for Using a Playbook

1. Be able to do at least five different play activities
2. Tolerate waiting for reinforcement
3. Understand that pictures represent objects
4. Have the motor and attending skills to seek out and bring back toys

To make a Playbook, use a child-sized loose-leaf notebook or photo album. The first page should have either a picture of the first activity or, if your child can read, the word for the activity. (Pictures and words can also be simultaneously presented in combination.) Each subsequent page will have another photo or word. Do not leave extra blank pages in this book; store them separately. Extra pages might distract your child if she flips to them and believes these activities are part of the current sequence she is supposed to complete.

In the beginning, activities in your child's Playbook should have a clear beginning and end so your child knows where to start and when to stop. For example, she might put a puzzle together or put blocks in a shape sorter. However, once she is skilled at the basic task, you can teach her to set a timer and do an activity such as coloring or looking at pictures until the buzzer sounds.

Activities in your child's Playbook should be things she knows how to do. In the early stages of learning to use the Playbook, they should also be things she enjoys doing. Later, you can add activities that are not quite as attractive but that are important for her to practice. For example, if she does not always enjoy talking to you, you might include a brief segment of conversation as part of her sequence of pictures, along with others that are more pleasurable. The last page should represent a reward your child can get for herself or request from you.

Your child works through the book in sequence. Start with one task and then the reward and gradually add more tasks. Provide minimal cues. At the start of the session say, "Do your Playbook." She is to open the book, touch the first photo, get the needed materials, put them on the table, and do the activity. When she finishes the activity, she puts the material away, turns the page, touches the picture, and gets the reward.

When your child is learning to use a Playbook, you will want to have the Playbook and play materials close at hand so she can easily find them. For example, the book might be on the table and the toy on a shelf near her seat. Minimize other distractions so she is not drawn off task by other items of potential interest. It is very important that you stand *behind* your child to prompt her, so that seeing you does not become part of her expectation for independent play. Do not speak to her to prompt her behavior, but use physical prompts and gestures to guide her though the steps. These prompts are much easier to fade (gradually reduce) than are verbal instructions.

When your child can do one sequence, add a second item, and as she masters that, a third, fourth, etc. For example, she might first color a picture, then assemble a puzzle, put pegs in a pegboard, and finally get her reinforcement.

When your child can do several items consistently, you can move the materials farther away so she has to travel a bit to get to them. You can also build in social and communicative opportunities (McClannahan & Krantz, 1999). For example, if one activity is coloring with crayons, the next page might cue her to pick up the picture and bring it to you, saying, "Look what I did." Similarly, if she built a tower of blocks, the next card might cue her to come to you, take you by the hand, and say, "Come see what I did" or "Come," if her speech is more limited. If your child uses an augmentative communication system such as a communication board she can use this equipment to communicate with you. Another way to build in social interaction is to include some activities where two children do the same task at the same time. One activity for your child might be to approach her sibling with a particular toy or game and say, "Let's play."

As the Playbook becomes longer and more complex, you can insert several reinforcements at different points in the sequence. You can include social reinforcement, such as the praise she gets from you when she brings you a picture to admire. You can also use a token system, if that is helpful for your child. The tokens can be exchanged for something she wishes to "buy" at the end of the session. Be sure to vary the order of the activities so she has to pay attention to the book and not just memorize a sequence.

Playbooks are powerful tools for helping children learn to do a series of independent activities. For a detailed description of using this type of visual prompt for teaching many activities in addition to play, see the fine book by autism experts Lynn McClannahan and Patricia Krantz, *Activity Schedules for Children with Autism* (Woodbine House, 1999). They describe in detail how to set up a schedule and teach your child to use it without becoming prompt dependent.

Pretend Play

Pretend play or "make believe" is a hallmark of childhood play and one of the more daunting skills for children with autism to master. Your step-by-step work with your child can pay off in important ways if you lay a good foundation for pretend play. Pretend play can contribute to high quality social interactions. It can also give your child the opportunity to "stand in the shoes" of others such as a mommy, police officer, or teacher. Playing these roles may give her some empathy for the experiences of these other people. Learning empathy is a challenge for people with autism and we should seek as many avenues as possible to support this learning.

In this section, we will describe five different levels of programs for teaching pretend play (Table 2-12). Many children with autism will be able to learn all of these pretend skills. They are valuable for early and middle childhood. If an older child beyond the age of ten or eleven has not learned them, however, we would probably focus instead on acting out "skits" of social interactions or on sports, because these are more age appropriate skills for teens and young adults.

Table 2-12 | Levels of Pretend Play

+ Pretend Nonverbal Imitation
+ Pretend Receptive Actions
+ Pretend Complex Receptive Actions
+ Pretend Representational Play
+ Pretend Joint Imitative Play Including Play Narration

Pretend Imitation

You have already taught your child various nonverbal imitations, which have helped her learn skills for interactive pretend play. For example, you have taught her to imitate your rolling a truck or feeding a doll. You will now use these same skills to introduce the fantasy aspect of play.

Table 2-13 summarizes the skills a child should master before pretend imitation training. One of these is the ability to imitate two-step use of toys. For example, your child should be able to stack two blocks or put a block in a cup and then dump it out. She should also have mastered gross motor imitations, such as clapping or stamping her feet, and be able to put several of these actions into a chain, such as clapping, touching her head, and

> **Table 2-13** | Prerequisites for Pretend Imitation Play
>
> ◆ Be able to imitate using toys
> ◆ Do two-step imitation with toys
> ◆ Do gross motor nonverbal imitation
> ◆ Chain several gross motor imitations in a series
> ◆ Optional—be capable of verbal imitation

touching her toes. If she is capable of verbal imitation, that will enrich her pretend play, because it will make it easier to share the development of a story with her play partner. However, children without speech can still learn to enjoy simple pretend sequences such as feeding a doll or putting the doll to sleep. As their language develops, they can then build on these skills to develop more complex pretend play.

To teach imitation of pretend actions, first select a toy or activity. If you use toys and other items that have intrinsic appeal for your child, this makes it more likely that she will enjoy the sessions and want to be with you. For example, if she likes dolls, fire trucks, or chalk boards, these would all be useful items. However, do not use toys that she enjoys primarily for rote or stereotypic activity, because it may be hard to distract her from this activity. For example, if she turns the fire truck over to spin the wheels, this would not be a suitable toy for learning pretend imitation.

Sit facing your child and say, "Do this" as you play with a toy. For example, use a toy comb to comb your hair or put a doll in a car. When she imitates, reinforce her and go on to the next trial. Teach your child some pretend actions that involve objects and some that do not. For example, you can do the action of pretending to run by standing up and jogging in place or pretend to sleep by closing your eyes and putting your head on your folded hands.

Initially, you will do one- or two-step imitations and then gradually add steps. For example, you could drive a toy school bus out of the garage, open the door, and put a doll inside, then drive the bus to another location and take the doll out. Then drive the bus back to the garage. This sequence could be extended to pick up several children along the way, and, if your child is verbal, she could learn to greet the doll as he boards the bus. Similarly, she could take a toy electric razor out of a kit bag, pretend to shave with it just like Daddy, put it back in the bag, and take out a play bottle of after shave lotion and pretend to put some on. If your child has speech, you could end the sequence by having her say, "Looking good!"

Pretend Receptive Actions

After your child can imitate pretend actions, you can teach her the labels that go with the actions and help her discriminate among labels for pretend actions. Table 2-14 indicates that to learn this skill she should be able to imitate your pretend acts, follow receptive commands such as "Show me the ball" or "Give me the cup," and follow receptive action commands such as "Jump" or "Run." (*Receptive commands* provide your child with a concrete object such as a book or a cup to manipulate, while *receptive action commands* require your child to engage in an action without an enduring concrete cue as to what she is to do.) Because there is no object to manipulate, receptive action commands can be difficult for some children. Youngsters who have trouble following these action commands may need a photographic cue to help them remember what they are supposed to do.

To teach receptive commands for pretend play, seat your child in a chair facing yours. Say, "Pretend you are _____." For

---

Table 2-14 | Prerequisites for Pretend Receptive Play Actions

1. Imitate nonverbal pretend play
2. Follow your receptive commands
3. Follow commands for receptive action labels
   (e.g., "show me jump")

example, "Pretend you are sleeping" or "Pretend you are feeding the doll." If your child does as you ask, reinforce her as appropriate. Otherwise, prompt her by silently modeling the pretend imitation. Go on to the next trial. Initially, your child may not understand what "pretend" means. For some children this will begin as just another receptive command such as "get the ball," or "show me jumping." Understanding will follow from practice.

Be sure you have multiple toys available so that your child has to discriminate among them to select the one that is appropriate. For example, you might have a doll and spoon, a comb, and a toy car. If your child has problems with receptive discriminations, stick to instructions that involve the use of toys rather than gestures alone. For example, she will find it easier if you say, "Pretend to put the doll to sleep on the bed" rather than "Pretend to sleep," as the objects (doll and bed) and additional words (doll and bed) may provide extra clues about exactly what is expected. You may also need to build from one or two activities to several so that the initial discriminations are simple ones.

Pretend: Complex Receptive

After your child learns simple receptive pretend commands, you can teach her more sustained pretend play and continue building her receptive discrimination skills. The prerequisites for complex receptive pretending are listed in Table 2-15 on the next page.

To teach complex receptive pretend skills, sit facing your child and give an instruction such as, "Pretend to let the doll drive the car, and have her drive it into the garage." Later, you can make the sequence increasingly elaborate with steps such as, "Pretend to have the doll drive the car, then have her drive it to the garage, then have her put gas in the car, and then drive away." Keep a record of the percentage of correct trials.

If your child has trouble following complex receptive commands, you can help by having a series of photographs of the actions that you request. For example, there could be photos of putting the doll in the car and of the car being pushed into the

Table 2-15 | Prerequisites for Pretend Complex Receptive Actions

1. Be able to imitate nonverbal receptive pretend actions (e.g., imitating feeding a doll)
2. Follow receptive commands for pretend actions (e.g., feeding a doll when asked to do so)
3. Do a chain of several nonverbal pretend actions (e.g., imitating putting a cow in a barn, putting a pig in the barn, pushing the tractor)
4. Do a chain of several receptive pretend actions (e.g., putting the people on an airplane, rolling the plane down the runway, and flying in the sky in response to the request to "Put the people on the plane, make it roll on the runway, and fly in the sky.")

garage. Be sure to adjust the pace of instruction to your child's ability to process the information.

Pretend: Representational Play

Pretending to be what we are not is one of the pleasures of childhood play. Children use a cardboard box as a spaceship or a couple of fallen logs as a fort. They pretend to be astronauts, puppy dogs, or teachers.

For children with autism, learning representational play skills builds more abstract pretend play skills, helps them generalize their receptive actions, and is a cornerstone in the foundation for typical play behavior. Remember, by "generalize" we mean to transfer a skill to different settings and objects with various people. The receptive play skills your child learned in earlier programs will be generalized to more varied play settings and become part of actual play interactions as she masters pretend representational play.

Most children with autism do not engage spontaneously in this kind of play and may not enjoy doing it "just for fun," but they can sometimes learn at least the rudiments of what we call representational play. We find that some children eventually do enjoy this play, while others do not. Those children who learn representational play and come to enjoy it have made a major step into the mainstream of childhood. Youngsters who acquire the skills, but do not enjoy them can still enter into some childhood situations more skillfully than they did before. Children who do not learn these skills will have some significant limits on their ability to be part of the social interaction of early and middle childhood, although they may well find other ways, such as through sports and computer games, to join with their peers.

As you see in Table 2-16, a child is ready to learn this program when she can follow receptive commands, imitate pretend actions, and engage in receptive pretend skills. Each of these has already been described in this chapter.

Table 2-16 | Prerequisites for Pretend Presentational Play

1. Be able to imitate nonverbal receptive pretend actions
2. Follow receptive commands for pretend actions
3. Have mastered complex receptive play actions

To teach the basics of representational play, sit facing each other with an object on the table. For example, you might have a plastic banana on the table and say, "Pretend this is a telephone." You would model the skill by holding the banana to your ear and saying, "Hello." Gradually introduce more objects and have several on the table at once. For example, you might have a plastic box and say, "Pretend this is a car" and a stick and box might be introduced with "Pretend this is a drum." A tongue depressor with a face drawn on it and piece of tissue paper could be accompanied by the instruction to "Pretend to put the doll to bed and cover her up." You can also have representational play without objects. For example, you could say to your child, "Pretend you are a kitty cat," and model the meow of a cat as you crawl on all fours!

If your child has problems grasping the abstract concepts that are part of representational play, you might first teach it with photographic cues. For example, show her a picture of someone pretending that a banana is a telephone.

Initially teach representational play skills on a trial-by-trial basis. Reinforce your child for correct responses, and prompt correct responses. In the initial stages of mastering a new skill, you should heavily reinforce your child even if she requires prompts to respond. After the initial stages of learning a new skill, however, reinforce prompted responses only with positive feedback (e.g., "right,") and give your child much more praise and reinforcement for unprompted correct responses.

Pretend: Joint Imaginary Play

When we think about play, it is often in the context of two or more children. We have probably all pretended to be a parent and baby, teacher and student, doctor and patient. The skills involved in joint imaginary play require your child to use interactive play skills, use her pretend skills in an interactive and natural format, and give her opportunities to generalize information she learns in other contexts.  For example, she may have studied "community helpers" and can pretend to be a physician, police officer, or fire fighter.

Table 2-17 lists the prerequisites to learn joint imaginary play.

Start by sitting next to your child and saying, "Let's pretend that ____" and enact a sequence in which both partners have an equal role. For example, you might say, "Let's pretend that we're playing school. I'll be the teacher and you be the child." It's important that you each have an equal role so your child can learn the

Table 2-17 | Prerequisites for Joint Imaginary Pretend Play

1. Have mastered pretend representational play
2. Be able to take turns
3. Be familiar with information about daily activities in the community (e.g., what does a police officer do; what happens in a supermarket, on the playground, at the dentist's office)

give-and-take that is characteristic of most conversations in real life. Each sequence should be four to eight minutes long and each participant should be describing her activities as she goes along.

Some children have a good enough sense of the required steps in these play sequences that, with a little prompting, they can follow your play suggestions and respond to your initiations. For example, in the teacher and child scenario you might say "I'm the teacher and I'm going to ask you to go to the blackboard and write your ABCs. You can pretend that you don't know how to write some letters and ask me to help."

Other children need more help. You might provide a prewritten script (perhaps from watching a videotape) that your child can follow. This little "mini-play" would have lines for both partners and sometimes the child could play one role and sometimes the other. Or you could give your child a sequence of pictures showing her what to do and prompting her speech. For example, the photographs might show a physician picking up a stethoscope and holding it to the doll that is held in its "mother's" arms. There might also be a picture of the doll getting a "shot" and the "mother" comforting her baby.

It helps if the initial play sequences are about activities that are part of your child's daily life, such as getting food at the store, delivering mail, or playing school.

After your child engages in joint imaginary play with one other child, you will introduce a third person and then a fourth. Other children are not nearly as predictable play partners as are adults, and you need to prepare your child for this. You can, for example, play your own pretend roles in many different ways so she learns there is no single script for any given play scenario. As soon as she has learned a new script, you should introduce variations, to make it a bit unpredictable. If your child still has problems using pretend play with other children, you might provide some coaching by whispering in her ear some ways to respond to the variation in theme. This would best be done with the cooperation of a playmate who is very patient and who does not mind pausing from time to time.

Play Narration

Learning how to talk about what we are doing as we play is another ability that emerges in childhood. In fact, typical children spend a great deal of time during play narrating what they are doing or what they see others doing.

Learning the skills of play narration helps your child increase the duration and complexity of her play skills and improves her expressive language skills. According to Table 2-18, to work on these skills, she needs to be able to engage in parallel play and sustained independent play, use Play Stations, and have advanced language, including sentences with nouns, verbs, prepositions, and adjectives. For all of these programs, keep data on how long the play session lasts and how many prompts you have to give your child during the session.

Narrating Your Child's Play. Your teaching progression in introducing play narration is first to narrate your child's play

---

Table 2-18 | Prerequisites for Play Narration

1. Have mastered parallel play
2. Have mastered sustained independent play
3. Have mastered Play Stations
4. Have completed a variety of advanced language programs
   or have mastered advanced language skills without
   special programs

while she plays, then to have her narrate your play, and finally to have her narrate her own play. To begin, say to your child, "You play and I'll tell a story." You would then narrate your child's actions. For example, in the first stage as she plays with a barnyard set, you might say, "You are a farmer and you put on the farmer's hat. You are taking the animals out of the barn and putting them in the yard. You are putting the man on the back of the horse and he is riding, trot trot, trot. You put the horse back in the barn and it goes 'neigh.' Then you put the cow away and it goes 'moo.'"

At first, your child's play may be part of a written or modeled script that she has followed many times in imitation of you. As you introduce new toys and provide essential prompts, she should be able to broaden the array of toys she uses and how she arranges them. She should also be able to engage in appropriate play behaviors for sustained periods of time. If your child is slow to generalize, keep adding more toys and scripts. Most children who have progressed this far through the sequence will eventually be able to generalize to some new play.

The major goal of this initial program is to increase appropriate play. This makes it important to redirect self-stimulation or other inappropriate play with gestural or verbal prompts. If your child struggles to come up with play ideas, you should also gently guide her in the direction of appropriate play. For example, you could say, "What about the airplane?"

Having Your Child Narrate Your Play. In the next teaching sequence, your child narrates your play. This is an opportunity to increase her spontaneous speech, improve her ability to stick to a single topic, and expand her ability to narrate across a variety of play scenarios.

To begin this interaction say, "I'll play and you tell a story." You can help your child by asking her specific questions about the story in the beginning. For example, "What am I doing with the cow?" Later you will ask more general questions such as, "What is happening now?"

At first, you may use the same materials that were used in the previous program. This strategy provides two advantages.

First, your child will be familiar with those materials. Second, your child will have already heard a great deal of narration regarding these items. This may help her in formulating her narrative sentences. In addition, if you used materials that were entirely new to your child, she might become frustrated at not being able to play with them herself. In the beginning, your child's narration may sound a lot like yours. That's fine for a start. You can add new toys and new activities that will require her to expand her narration.

Having Your Child Narrate Her Play. In the final sequence, your child narrates her own play. For some children, this step from narrating your play to narrating her own will come easily. For other children, the program will have to be taught in a systematic fashion as you have taught the prior steps.

In providing systematic instruction for play narration, it is important to increase both the duration and the breadth of your child's play. While it may be enticing to build the duration of this skill with one toy or scene, this may be counterproductive. It is probably best to work on increasing duration across many tasks and toys. For example, rather than focusing on getting your child to describe the barn sequence for longer and longer periods of time, you should branch out and include airports, rockets, and school buses. Using a variety of toys will make it easier for your child to generalize the skill. After your child is able to play for a specific duration (say, thirty seconds) with at least ten familiar (taught) scenes and five novel scenes, you may target a new, longer duration (say, forty-five seconds).

It is possible to teach several different play narration formats (i.e., child narrating, parent narrating) simultaneously, but this is not recommended in the initial stages of the program. Your child should be able to play appropriately with you narrating for at least three minutes across a wide and random variety of materials, before you introduce the format of your child narrating the play activity.

While your goals will vary based on your child's age and characteristics, it is generally reasonable to expect that your child will eventually be able to narrate for ten minutes. Keep in mind that your child's initial periods of narration might be as brief as fifteen seconds. You will increase duration as your child achieves mastery. Mastery in this context refers to meeting the criteria for the target length of time with no prompts or redirections, and across multiple tasks (including novel presentations of items). That is, your child will narrate a play scenario for the specified amount of time, including with materials she has never played with before, without any guidance from you.

Summary

It is vitally important to teach play skills to children with autism because they rarely develop appropriate or adaptive play skills without highly systematic teaching. Untutored, their play skills often appear odd and can be stigmatizing. Children with autism need help in developing solitary play skills, parallel play skills, and cooperative play skills.

Play skills represent a powerful bridge to developing relationships with others and can be a focus of instruction from the earliest stages of ABA programming. The complexity and breadth of play skill programming is substantial. Your child's progress will be made in incremental steps, with a focus on monitoring progress and assessing readiness for more advanced programs.

Parents and teachers should remember that play places enormous demands on many children with autism, and may not be intrinsically motivating for some time to come. Putting some thought and energy into motivating and reinforcing your child will increase your success in teaching her these skills.

References

Cox, R. (1993). Normal childhood development from birth to five years. In E. Schopler, M. E. Van Bourgondien, & M.M. Bristol (Eds.), *Preschool issues in autism* (pp. 39-57). New York, NY: Plenum Press.

Harris, S. L. & Weiss, M. J. (1998). *Right from the start: Behavioral intervention for young children with autism.* Bethesda, MD: Woodbine House.

McClannahan, L. E. & Krantz, P. J. (1999). *Activity schedules for children with autism.* Bethesda, MD: Woodbine House.

3 | Teaching the Language of Social Skills

The Kimball Family Teaches Scott to Share

It was not an easy teaching session. Scott Kimball was in one of his "moods" and did not want to share any of his toys with his sister, Rita. When she asked for the dump truck, he whined and turned his back on her. When she reached for the ambulance, he pushed her away and she fell backwards, bumping against the arm of the sofa and starting to cry. Allison called an early halt to the playtime. She redirected Scott to another activity to calm him down, then comforted Rita.

Scott had been getting increasingly aggressive with Rita in the past few weeks. The Kimballs talked at length with their home consultant, Matt Becker, about this problem. Matt pointed out that in some ways this obnoxious behavior was a positive thing. It wasn't OK for Scott to push and ignore Rita, and he could not be allowed to hurt her. But the aggressive behavior signified that Scott was increasingly interested in the toys and wanted them for himself. That interest in play was the positive change! If Scott could learn some social rules, he could combine his pleasure in toys with more appropriate interactions with his sister. His current problematic behavior gave his parents the opportunity to teach him how to share and follow the rules that are important in childhood play.

Matt emphasized to the Kimballs that although they might use redirection when Scott was aggressive, that alone was not enough to teach him what he needed to learn. The key to success was developing positive behaviors to cope with situations in which he had to share toys. The Kimballs introduced a "sharing" program in which Scott got a lot of practice at giving a toy to Rita and then having her return it to him. He learned to say, "We share" when he wanted her to give back a toy after a few minutes. They also started a "take turns" program to help Scott learn to let Rita go first some of the time while he waited for his turn. Good waiting was rewarded with praise and tokens that he later cashed in for treats. To be fair to both children, Rita also earned tokens to buy treats for herself.

Not only did Scott have to learn these rules of patience and sharing in childhood play, he also needed a number of other skills to become an attractive playmate. For example, it was difficult for him to keep up a conversation with Rita. He had started to say, "Let's play" when he wanted to play with her, but after she said "Okay," he did not know what to say next. Her efforts to sustain the talk would usually peter out after a couple of rounds because Scott did not understand the importance of reciprocating her efforts. So, once the aggressive behavior was under better control and their play sessions had again become pleasurable, the Kimballs began to work on increasing Scott's ability to sustain an exchange with Rita.

What Does the Kimball Family Experience Mean for You?

Children with autism not only have to learn how to use toys and play sports, they also have to learn the many social rules involved in playing with and being with other children. There are myriad rules to learn and Scott needed many lessons to help him master these social expectations. Some of the lessons were harder for him than others.

Scott's whining and pushing his sister were not unusual for a child with autism who is gaining in social awareness and play skills. No longer indifferent to Rita and to his toys, he had times when he wanted to control the toys and not share with her. Younger typically developing children sometimes do the same thing. Most young children get into scuffles, cry, lash out, or have tantrums when

things don't go their way. Learning to follow the rules and tolerate frustration and disappointment takes time and effort.

Sometimes special skills also need to be taught to play partners. For example, playmates may need to learn to gain the attention of their play partner, to persist in their efforts to interact, or to provide feedback when their friend has responded to them. These skills will make peers more successful in their interactions with the child with autism.

Scott's social problems were not limited to inappropriate pushing and whining. He also lacked a number of positive behaviors that help to "grease the social wheel." He did not understand how to sustain a conversation, make a request of another child and accept that child's right to decline to share, or ask for information that he needed as part of their play together. Each of these had to be taught.

Scott needed help with nonverbal behaviors as well. These included such things as giving a "high five" and making other gestures, and understanding how far to stand from other children so as not to invade their space. Similarly, he needed to learn the slang expressions used by his peers. His sister was a good resource for "in" expressions, because, as every parent knows, childhood vocabulary changes with each generation. What adults might think of as the "right" way to talk could be very "wrong" to other kids.

Your child's use of social skills "language" may be much like Scott's, or it may differ in important ways. Some of the material in this chapter will be helpful to almost every child, and you can select programs that best match your child's needs. As was the case for play skills in Chapter Two, be certain that your child has the basic skills well established before you teach more advanced ones. Even if your child engages in a behavior once in a while, do not assume he has mastered it.

If your child is nonverbal, there are still skills in this chapter that will be relevant for him. Remember that communication is both verbal and nonverbal, and that expression can take many forms besides verbal communication. For example, we will address how to teach children to recognize and understand the nonverbal communication of others. We will also describe some ways to use pictures or words to facilitate communication.

What Is the Language of Social Skills?

As shown in Table 3-1, we are using the term "language of social skills" for a variety of verbal and nonverbal behaviors. Appropriate social behavior includes the use of polite terms such as "please" and "thank you." It also requires a child to understand that he should respond to an adult differently than to a child, and that how he acts at home may not be acceptable "in company." He must master a variety of rules that adults place on children's conduct, such as not hitting other children, not whining at play, not knocking down other children's creations, not throwing a ball indoors, and on and on.

Playing games with other children requires sharing of information. This giving and getting of information is essential to the progress of play. For example, a little girl tells her brother, "This is the mommy doll and this is the daddy doll." That shared as-

---

Table 3-1 | The Language of Social Skills

- ◆ Appropriate social behavior
- ◆ Following social rules
- ◆ Getting and giving information
- ◆ Maintaining a conversation
- ◆ Slang, idioms, and expressions
- ◆ Telling jokes
- ◆ Using gestures

---

sumption then lets them progress to the next step in their play. He might say, "I'm gonna be the daddy, and you be the mommy."

Scott illustrated well the problems that some children with autism have in maintaining a conversation. A child may know how to initiate a social bid ("Will you play ball with me?") but, after the other child agrees, does not know what to say next. During their play, children maintain a running dialog with one another ("Know what?" "What?" "I'm gonna move them guys over there." "OK, and I'll put this big guy in the middle. Right there. Smacko"). The child with autism must learn this fine art of dialog.

Every generation has its own slang words. "Get a life" is currently popular among young people in the U.S. and may be accompanied by the rolling of one's eyes. Their parents' generation had their own way of conveying exasperation to adults. Each culture and society also has its own idioms and expressions. The term "feeling blue" is commonly used in the U.S. to indicate sadness, but the term would be puzzling to a person coming here from West Africa. Even within the United States there are variations such as referring to a sweet-tasting carbonated beverage as "soda" in some areas and "pop" in others. People with autism, even those who are very bright, often have a hard time learning not to take idioms literally. For example, we know a young man who was perplexed by the expression, "It is raining cats and dogs."

Telling jokes is another important childhood skill. ("What did one wall say to the other wall?" "Meet you at the corner.")

Children need to learn what is funny, how to be funny, and how to appreciate humor. This includes both formal joke telling and the more informal commentaries they make in their social group. This informal humor includes the remarks they make about adults, and the sometimes unfortunate things they say about one another. A related skill that children need to learn is when it is acceptable to laugh at someone's misfortune and when this behavior would appear mean-spirited. For example, it is funny when a character in a cartoon gets bonked on the head or stubs his toe. When someone is truly hurt, however, it is not funny.

As we noted in the case of Scott, not all information sharing is through words. Gestures are an integral part of communication. We need to coordinate gestures with words and we need to know when we should be looking at another person. If Rita tells Scott, "Gimme that," and points toward a toy truck, the information will not be useful unless Scott understands that he must follow her gesture as well as listen to her words. Some gestures of childhood are necessary for communication and some are essential to fit in with other children. The "high five" and "low five" are the best current examples of such gestures in the United States and many other English-speaking parts of the world, but children in different communities develop their own distinctive nonverbal vocabulary. A child who cannot understand and offer these gestures is marked as an outsider by other children.

The Development of the Language of Social Skills

Just as motor skills, speech, and play skills all evolve through childhood, so too does a person's understanding of the language of social skills.

Children typically learn the rudiments of controlling their anger and aggression, as well as to take turns and share, as toddlers and preschoolers. The young child needs adult support and help in controlling feelings and mastering impulses. Adults can help him regain his composure, put his distress into words, and find solutions for his problems. Sometimes this process may involve a short time-out or other mild consequence, but most importantly, the child is helped to regain control and find a way to resolve a problem. For the one-year-old child, this adult intervention may simply involve distraction with another attractive toy. For the older child, it may mean working out a way to share a desirable item or a reminder that his turn will be next. This parental involvement is important not only to resolve the conflict of the moment, but also to teach the child how to deal with strong feelings and solve interpersonal problems. Parents of preschool children spend a great deal of time in this rule teaching.

Aggressive Behavior. The aggressive behavior of the one-year-old or two-year-old is not hostile in nature. A child this young may want a toy that another child has and push or shove to get it. But, his goal is not to harm the other child or to express dislike of the other child. He only wants to get the toy. For older children, aggression may not only have the goal of getting to a desirable object, it may also be designed to express feelings about another child. For example, a girl may hit her brother if she resents how much parental attention he is getting.

By the age of six or seven years, children use less physical aggression and more verbal aggression to get their way. They use name-calling ("Fatso," "Four-eyes") and threats ("You'll be sorry") in place of punches and kicks. Children this age are also increasingly able to resolve their disputes by talking with one another. Over time, they need less adult intervention to help them control their anger because they are able to settle their squabbles themselves.

Telling Jokes. Humor, too, develops with age. A very young child understands that there are things called jokes and that people tell them and laugh. In his effort to emulate this humor, the three-year-old will announce that he is telling a joke, say some nonsense words or a word that he thinks is terribly funny, and burst into laugher. He is delighted if you join him. His sense of humor will soon grow subtler. For example, Molly, a four-year-old we know, was playing a word game with her grandmother that involved naming all the words she could think of that started with "p." Later in the day she came to her grandmother with a serious expression on her face and announced that she had another "p" word. Then she said "crocodile" and burst into laughter. She was showing an appreciation of the radical shift in perspective that creates humor.

Young children also love "slap-stick," the physical clowning that is so clear in its humorous intent. In the early elementary school years, children come to appreciate the incongruity of humor and plays on words. "Knock-knock" jokes are classics of childhood joke telling. The subtlety of humor evolves with age. ("Knock, knock." "Who's there?" "Ida" "Ida who?" "Idaho")

Conversational Exchange. Our ability to engage in a sustained conversation begins in infancy. Our first conversations are the little verbal games that parents play with their babies. The sounds, nods, smiles, and other facial gestures that pass back and forth between infant and caretaker are a template for later verbal exchange.

The typically developing toddler uses single words to express basic requests and observations. "Mama" can mean, "I want Mama," "I see Mama," "Mama, give me the ball," and so forth. The two-year-old is building two-word phrases such as "Mommy go" to mean "Mommy went away" or "Mommy leave me, do it myself." The complexity of speech increases at a marked pace over the next several years. The six-year-old can say things such as, "Sally took the doll from under the table and I got the ball and bounced it over to Lee."

As the grammatical complexity of a child's language increases, so too does his ability to carry his own end of a conversation. Initially, it takes a great deal of work from the adult to sustain a conversation with the child. As the child gets older, he reciprocates with an adult more skillfully, and can carry on a conversation with a peer.

Conversations with peers occur later, because children are not as aware of the need to create a supportive structure for sustaining the exchange. In fact, this is one of the reasons children with autism have a harder time conversing with peers than with adults. Adults have a very nuanced ability to recognize the needs of the child with autism and provide the right prompts. A child, no matter how well intentioned, will not understand how to do this and after a few attempts may give up on the dialog.

In Chapter Four, we discuss another aspect of conversational exchange that is problematic for children with autism. This is the ability to adopt the perspective of other people and be sensitive to their needs and concerns. The remainder of the present chapter describes teaching programs that can help you teach your child with autism to develop improved abilities in the language of social skills.

Teaching the Language of Social Skills

Most children with autism require intensive programming in the language of social skills over several years. Even if children no longer need highly structured intervention in other areas, they often require ongoing instruction in the social realm.

Children with autism are doubly challenged in learning the language of social skills. First, they struggle with understanding social information and with learning how to interact with peers. Second, understanding and using complex language is a significant challenge for many of them. As a result, learning to manage social interaction often presents formidable language demands along with the so-  cial ones. Because of this, our social skills programming addresses both the social skills and the language skills that a child needs to be successful in social interactions.

Although we are reviewing a variety of critical skills in this chapter, remember that there are an essentially limitless number of language-based social skills. Your child will need more help with certain skills and situations than with others. However, if you master the instructional approach we are describing, you may be able to create your own programs to teach new skills as the need arises. In addition, the professionals who work with your child (e.g., teacher, speech-language therapist, behavior analyst) should be very helpful in this area. They may be able to provide you with programming ideas and a list of commercially available resources. We have also listed a variety of commercially available curricular materials and games for teaching social skills in Appendix A.

This chapter, unlike those on play skills and perspective taking, does not present a sequence of skills. Instead, it offers multiple targets (goals/objectives) of instruction, and you can teach several skills simultaneously. It is important to assess your child's readiness for each of the skills presented and to work with your child's educators to choose appropriate targets.

Many of the skills we review can be taught using discrete trial instruction and incidental teaching strategies. Incidental teaching, as described in Chapter One, uses naturally occurring events to teach skills and to help children provide more elaborate communicative responses. There are also a number of additional strategies that are particularly relevant for teaching social skills. These strategies, including role plays, Social Stories (Gray, 1993), Comic Strip Conversations (Gray, 1994), rule cards, and videotape segments, will be discussed at several points in the chapter (Table 3-2).

Appropriate Social Behavior

One of the first challenges for a child with autism is learning basic social behaviors. Typically developing children pick up much of this information informally by observing other children and copying them. They are also extremely responsive to feedback from adults. This ability to learn by watching and to be mo-

Table 3-2 | Strategies for Teaching Social Skills

1. Role Plays

- Can be done with characters (dolls, puppets) or with people
- May involve your child as observer and/or as participant
- Critical tasks include identifying skills and rectifying problems in interaction

2. Social Stories

- Used to convey information about multi-element social tasks
- Can be modified to include illustrations, to assist in comprehension
- Multiple versions may assist in generalizing knowledge
- Comprehension assessment may be desirable
- Might be extended to target multi-element tasks and to address fears and challenging behaviors

3. Comic Strip Conversations

- Useful strategy for building conversational skills
- Helpful in generalizing skills

4. Videotape Segments

- Useful tool for identifying appropriate behavior in self and peers
- Provides opportunities to reinforce appropriate social behavior
- Can assist children in identifying behaviors (their own and peers') that are inappropriate
- Can be used in conjunction with role plays to work on areas of difficulty

5. Rule Cards

- Provide a visual reminder of activity-specific rules
- Provide a brief review of rules just prior to activity
- Can be easily linked to token economies, to provide rewards for following rules

tivated by adult approval makes social learning appear "spontaneous" for the typical child.

Children with autism are less interested in observing peers, and often are not very responsive to adult instruction. As a result, they require systematic instruction to understand what is expected in the realm of social behavior. A good place to begin that teaching is with conventional responses.

Table 3-3 | Appropriate Social Behaviors

- Conventional responses
- Responding to common occurrences
- Sharing materials and toys
- Managing frustration appropriately
- Assertiveness

Conventional Responses. Conventional responses (Table 3-3) are the "pardon me," "whoops," "nice to meet you" things that we say throughout the day. The rules for using them are generally clear and many of these routine social opportunities present themselves over the course of a day. Unfortunately, children with autism are often indifferent to these events. If they are to learn to recognize and use these opportunities, we need to teach the necessary skills.

One target of conventional response is the use of greetings and other "social niceties." For example, it is important that your child greets and says goodbye to peers by name. This is one way to build a social connection, and to spark other children's interest in interacting with your child.

To teach this conventional response, we separate it into two components. One component is recognizing the identity of the other child and the second is making the appropriate response to that child. These skills may need to be taught separately, with an initial focus on identifying peers. Begin by selecting a small group of children for your child to call by name. For example, it may be most important to learn the names of peers sitting in his area of the classroom or those assigned to his reading group. Initially, your child can rehearse these names with photos using a discrete trial format, then he can practice them at circle time and be prompted to use them in class.

In teaching responses, the emphasis should be on reciprocity. Children with autism need to reply when someone initiates an interaction with them. It is helpful to focus on greetings, responses to simple inquiries such as "How are you?" and farewells. It is usually best to target these skills in a discrete trial format with an instructor before using them with peers or in an incidental context. It is generally best to teach as naturalistically as possible. For example, your child may be asked, "How are you?" at the beginning of each session and/or by different instructors at various times of the day (rather than have one instructor ask him repeatedly how he is).

Common Occurrences. Your child should also be taught to reply appropriately to other common social circumstances, such as when someone coughs or falls. Failure to respond to these events is common among children with autism. It is important for them to tune into the behaviors and experiences of their peers. The ability to respond to common occurrences will open the door to more elaborate conversations with peers. It will also ensure that peers don't experience the child as someone who just "does his own thing."

Table 3-4 | Discrete Trial Format for Common Social Event

Sample instructional sequence:
Instructor: "Ahhhh…. choooo!" (exaggerated sneeze)
Child: "Bless you."
Instructor: "Thank you!" (or other social reinforcement)

Table 3-4 describes a sequence for responding to a sneeze. As the table suggests, instructors may first deal with this common social event in a contrived discrete trial instruction format. In this context, the teacher "fakes a sneeze" and reinforces the child for his response. (Initially, this response may be prompted or scripted by the instructor. The instructor may say, "Say 'Bless you.'" For some children, this level of assistance is only needed a few times. Other children may require a lot of practice with this type of help.) This instructional sequence, while artificial, highlights the event for the child. Through this teaching, sneezing becomes more salient, and is defined as an opportunity to interact with another person.

As your child masters this concept, the exaggerated quality of the sneeze is gradually reduced. Eventually, you can work on appropriate responses to sneezing outside of the discrete trial instruction sessions. For example, you can say, "What do you say?" if someone sneezes and your child does not react. Once your child responds routinely to such occurrences with adults, responses to children should be easy to foster. Table 3-5 lists some common occurrences that might be taught first in a discrete trial format and then naturalistically.

Table 3-5 | Common Social Occurrences

Sneezing ...... "Bless you."	Coughing .... "Are you okay?"
Laughing ..... "What's so funny?"	Ouch .... "What happened?"
"Uh oh" .... "What happened?"	Crying .... "What's wrong?"
Yawning .... "Are you tired?"	"Oh no!" ...... "What's wrong?"
"Help!" .... "Can I help you?"	

Sharing. In Chapter Two, when we discussed play skills, we suggested various ways to help children learn to tolerate sharing toys and materials. The ability to share is an important social skill. Even if your child has learned sharing under controlled conditions, he may need help extending that into sharing in naturally occurring contexts. He must learn to surrender toys to peers on request and to ask appropriately for toys from another child.

After teaching the skill in a formalized program, it is important to create many different situations that require sharing. At first, you can generalize sharing skills with neutral materials and with adults. (Neutral materials would include toys that your child plays with, but is not overly interested in. It is easier for children to share toys that are not their favorites than it is to share cherished toys.) After he learns to share less

valued items, you can include more attractive materials and involve other children. For example, for one child you might start with pegboards or puzzles and work up to sharing Legos, blocks, or art materials.

Alternatives to Aggression. Another basic social skill that is learned throughout childhood is managing frustration. As is the case for other social skills, managing aggression can be very difficult for some children with autism. As we reported in the vignette that opened this chapter, Scott Kimball was aggressive when playing with his sister. He needed to learn to express his frustration in more appropriate ways, and stop hurting his sister.

When we deal with problem behaviors such as aggression, we do so primarily by teaching a child "pro-social behaviors" (i.e., behaviors that foster the development and maintenance of social relationships) that allow him to solve a problem constructively. Often, this involves recognizing that language deficits are partly responsible for many problem behaviors. One reason that children with autism act aggressively is that they lack the skills to express their desires appropriately. Behavior problems often erupt in the absence of adequate communication skills. This makes a communication system a vital component of your child's program. It is essential that he have a means of expressing his needs. A comprehensive program, with input from a speech-language pathologist, should address this issue.

A common cause of aggression or tantrums in children with autism is that they are overwhelmed by demands for social interaction. One solution is teaching them to ask for a reduction in the social demands or a break from social engagement. Your child can learn to ask for a break or for quiet time. This skill is important whether or not your child has a vocal means of requesting a break. Picture cues and other nonverbal methods of requesting a break can be used by children who have little speech.

Aggression may also arise if a child has difficulty sharing the teacher's attention, especially if he is used to one-to-one instruction. He has to learn to request teacher attention in a group setting. It is essential that the function of your child's problem behavior be assessed, and that the treatment package addresses this function by teaching him an alternative solution. For example, if your child engages in aggressive behavior to gain teacher attention, he must be taught the language to use when seeking her attention. Being able to say, "help me" or "look at this" provides him with a functional, adaptive, and effective way of meeting his need.

In the initial stages of learning these skills, your child may still have difficulty waiting patiently. Over time, he will become more adept at waiting. At first, it is important for all team members to respond immediately to requests for help, attention, or a break. We want to reward him for asking for what he needs, and we want to "catch him being good." Over time, we can increase the delay in our response.

It should be noted that the causes of aggressive behavior are numerous and highly variable among children with autism. Table 3-6 includes examples of how problem behaviors in children with autism were analyzed and replaced with adaptive behaviors.

Chapter One touched briefly on functional assessments—that is, formal assessments to thoroughly analyze the reasons that a child persists in a problematic behavior. This type of assessment, although complex, can be essential in reducing aggression. For helpful background, several books with information on these topics are listed in Appendix B. However, most parents will need help from a behavior analyst in identifying the functions of be-

Table 3-6 | Analyzing Functions of Misbehavior

Adam has been having an adjustment problem to his new brother, Jake. Like many older siblings, he has experienced a loss of some parental attention. He has started swatting the baby. A functional assessment indicated that attention is likely to be the motivating factor behind this aggression. Adam needs to learn a better way to get his parents' attention.

Adam's parents teach him to ask for their attention by tapping their shoulder when they are busy. He also learns to ask them, "Can you play with me?" Adam now has adaptive and appropriate means of gaining his parents' attention. In the beginning stages of learning this skill, Adam's parents needed to respond immediately every single time Adam tapped them. Over time, Adam became able to tolerate slight delays in their attention.

Sometimes when Emily sits down to work at her table at school, she swipes all the materials off of the desk and falls to the floor. Her teachers try to get her to sit in her chair, but she is often in a full-blown tantrum. A functional assessment conducted by the school psychologist pointed to escape from task demand as the reason for her behavior. Emily needs to learn to ask for a break from demands in a more appropriate way. Her teaching team will begin introducing the use of a "break" card. This card says, "break please" and Emily will learn to hand it to her teacher to make her needs known. The teaching team members have also made some curricular modifications. Because the behavior happened most often in receptive language tasks, they are interspersing those tasks with easier ones.

Lisa is content to play by herself. Her sister, Jessica, is very persistent in trying to play with her, however. Sometimes, Lisa responds well to Jessica's initiations. At other times, she hits her sister. A functional assessment conducted by the behavior analyst responsible for the home program indicates that escape from social demand is the motivation for this behavior. Lisa is taught to ask her sister to leave her alone or to say "maybe later."

haviors and in developing a plan that matches those functions and teaches replacement skills.

Assertiveness. Another essential element of appropriate social behavior is the development of assertiveness. Children with autism may be victims of bullies if they don't learn to respond assertively. Especially if they spend many hours in adult-directed instruction, learning to do what adults ask, they may be too easily bossed around by peers.

There are a variety of ways to target assertiveness skills. One of the simplest methods is to focus on personal and objective information. This is a very concrete way to teach your child that it is important to assert his own knowledge. For example, as shown in Table 3-7, a teacher may deliberately greet your child by the wrong name so that he can learn to correct the error. Making deliberate errors in objective information is another good way to teach your child to speak up when he hears something that is

---

Table 3-7 | Sample Misstatements to Encourage Assertive Behavior

Personal Information
Instructor: "Hi, Joey"
Child: "I'm not Joey. I'm Peter."

Instructor: "You have a brother."
Child: "I don't have a brother. I have a sister."

Objective information
Instructor: "The sun is blue."
Child: "No. The sun is yellow."

Instructor: "Cows say woof woof."
Child: "No. Cows say moo."

Instructor: "Your shirt is pink."
Child: "My shirt is green."

wrong. For example, an adult may make an incorrect assertion about an obvious fact, such as "your hair is blue," and help your child learn to correct mistakes with the right facts.

After he has learned to challenge errors of fact, a child can start learning how to respond in situations in which he is being treated unfairly. Common unfair practices of childhood include taking items away, skipping turns, or breaking the rules of a game.

Table 3-8 lists some appropriate assertive responses for children when they are not being treated fairly. These can initially be practiced in a discrete trial format, but then must be shifted to naturalistic interactions. For example, you may deliberately break the rule of a game during a family activity, as opposed to during a teaching session. A teacher may skip your child in distributing cookies at snack time. As you move to more natural situations, you need to provide your child with assistance if he does not respond independently in this context. You might cue your child if a playmate breaks a rule in a game and he does not seem to notice. For example, you might ask him, "Was that fair?" or "Did he follow the rules?" You can also help your child to voice concern over the problem. You might say, "Tell him." Alternately, you might script it for him, saying, "Tell him you can't go twice."

Table 3-8 | Appropriate Assertive Responses to Unfair Treatment

"Give me a turn."

"It's my turn."

"Give that back, please."

"Hey, give that back."

"That's not yours. That's mine" (for personal property).

Following Social Rules

Following social rules is another domain in which children with autism often need special coaching. A challenge in teaching

them to recognize and follow these rules is that there are countless rules to be mastered. Rules are often specific to situations, and may differ from teacher to teacher or activity to activity. Children with autism may require specific instruction in understanding and following rules for many specific circumstances before they begin to show a general understanding of rules. The amount of time that this requires varies from child to child. Some children learn rules nearly instantaneously, while others need more practice. Some children will continue to need reminders of rules for a long time to come.

Because of the importance of learning to recognize and follow social rules, a number of different teaching strategies have been developed. We will review several of these, including Social Stories (Gray, 1993, 1994), Rule Cards, Motivational Systems, and Problem Solving.

Social Stories

In our work with children with autism, we have found the use of "social stories" to be a useful method for teaching social rules. Social stories are brief, written narratives about what will happen or how a child is expected to behave in a specific situation. These stories are written in simple language and capture the essence of a social behavior.

Carol Gray, an educator employed by a school system in Michigan, created social stories as a means to convey complex social information to children with autism (1993, 1994). Social stories are designed to provide information about specific social situations rather than simply to give rules for behavior, and Gray provides clear guidelines to this effect. She suggests that one directive (rule) statement be given for every three to five informative sentences that describe the situation or give perspective on behavior. Reading her book is helpful when learning to construct social stories.

Social stories provide information about social circumstances, about the many ways social events might be experienced, and about expectations for appropriate behavior. We have used Gray's concept both in her original social stories format and in modified versions of our own design.

In our own work, we often recommend that families create picture books to go along with the stories. For some children, photos are used. This sometimes is more appealing to the child, and often seems to help the child understand the intent of the story. We often write the story using the names of the actual people in the child's life. Each page in the book contains a line of text and an illustration. We suggest that families create a minimum of three to five versions of each story, to ensure a broadly based introduction to the concepts of the story and to prevent the child from memorizing the material without comprehension. In some cases, we recommend assessing the child's understanding of the story with worksheets.

We use social stories to target several types of skills, including tasks that have several different steps (multi-element tasks), and social situations that may shift and change as they are played out (multi-element social situations). We also use the stories for some children who are learning to control inappropriate behavior or who are fearful. Table 3-9 on the next two pages has a sample story for each of these four circumstances.

In our experience, it is helpful to provide repeated presentations of the social story. So, parents may read the story at reading times, while the teacher reviews it before circle time. Many teachers feel it is extremely helpful to review the social story prior to the activity you are addressing (e.g., circle time). Whenever the social story is targeting a challenging behavior, however, we teach the social story first outside of these circumstances. Only when the child has demonstrated that he understands the concepts might

---

Table 3-9 | Sample Social Stories

All of the following stories were written with the pronoun I. While it may sometimes be necessary to use the third person, we generally prefer first person.

A Social Story for a Multi-Element Task
Cleaning Up

When the bell rings, the teacher says it's time to clean up. Sometimes I am working when the bell rings. Sometimes I am playing. When the bell rings, I will put away all of my things. Then I will be ready for the next activity. Sometimes I will have to put away many things. Sometimes I will have just one thing to put away. I need to put everything away when the bell rings. My teacher will be proud of me when I clean up all of my things. I will be happy too, because I'll be ready for the next activity. I can remember to clean up when the bell rings.

A Social Story for a Multi-element Social Situation
Lining Up When the Bell Rings

When the teacher rings the bell, it is time to line up. Everyone walks to the blackboard and faces the door. I might be first in line. I might be last in line. I might be behind a boy. I might be behind a girl. It is important to stand an arm's length behind the person in front, so that everyone has space and is comfortable. I can remember how to line up when the bell goes off.

A Social Story for Reduction of Challenging Behavior
I'm Sad, I'm Mad

Sometimes when I want something, I have to wait. Sometimes I can't have it at all. Sometimes this makes me feel sad or mad. When I am

---

we use it to help him calm down. Cheri Meiners, author and mother of a child with autism, has created a series of social stories books that are nicely illustrated and address many of the common problems shown by children with autism (2000).

Unlike many of the other techniques we describe in this book, Gray's work does not yet have extensive research support. This makes it all the more important that you collect good data on the use of social stories with your child and be certain they are effective rather than continuing to use them without documenting sad, I can say, "I am sad," and take a deep breath. When I am mad, I can say, "I am mad," and take a deep breath. Maybe I can wait. Maybe I can have it later or tomorrow. I can remember to take a deep breath and stay calm. Everyone will be proud of me when I can stay calm.

A Social Story for Reduction of Fear
The Barber Shop

(Karen Wojtowicz (1996) wrote this story when she was a home programmer at the Douglass School at Rutgers University in New Brunswick, New Jersey. It was written for a student who was extremely afraid of going to the barbershop, and who engaged in severe avoidance behavior around this activity. Each sentence of the story had pictures associated with it.)

I like to go to the barbershop. I see a lot of cool things there. I see barber chairs. I see hairbrushes and combs. I see mirrors. I see hair dryers and curling irons. I see bottles of shampoo. I see scissors too. I can watch people getting their hair cut. Snip. Snip. Snip. I can get a drink of water when I go to the barbershop. I can sit in the barber chair. I can put on a cape. I can go into the shampoo room and get a shampoo. First, I will lie back in the shampoo chair. Then Karen will put water on my hair. Then she will put some shampoo on my hair and make bubbles. She will tickle my hair when she is washing it. Then we will dry my hair with a towel. After that, I will sit in the barber chair so Karen can brush my hair. Then she will start to cut my hair with a scissors. Snip, snip, snip. She will cut the sides of my hair and the back of my hair. I will hear the sound snip, snip, snip. Soon, she will be done. I will look in the mirror and see how great I look. Everyone will be so proud of me. When I am finished, I will go back to school. I can sing the barbershop song in the van. Going to the barbershop is fun.

their benefits. We do know individual children who have responded well to the stories, and because they are in widespread use, we feel it is important to include them here.

Rule Cards

Rule cards are another tool for helping children follow social rules that are associated with a particular activity. A rule card is created for a specific activity and clearly states (in words or with pictures) the behavioral expectations for that activity. As shown in Table 3-10, these rules should be clear and brief. Print the rules on small cards that a child may carry in his pocket or can be posted by his desk.

Table 3-10 | Sample Rule Cards

Rules for library

1. Speak only when necessary.
2. Speak in a whisper.
3. Choose one book to read for the entire period.
4. Raise my hand when I need the librarian.

Rules for reading group

1. Read aloud only when it is my turn.
2. Listen when my friends read.
3. Raise my hand if I have something to say or when I want to answer a question.
4. Wait to be called on to answer.
5. Use a pencil for the worksheet.

Motivational Systems

Motivational systems can be potent in helping children learn to follow social rules. If your child is using some form of token economy as a reward system for appropriate behavior, tokens can be given for following specific rules. For example, tokens may be awarded at the end of each classroom period for following classroom rules such as staying in one's seat, doing one's work, or listening to the teacher. At the end of the period, the teacher or shadow (a classroom "coach" for the child) can review with your child the extent to which the rules were followed, and give tokens accordingly.

This strategy can also be easily extended into self-monitoring, in which your child learns to evaluate for himself how well he followed the rules. When self-monitoring is used, your child can actually give tokens to himself. In the beginning stages of this approach, bonus tokens may be given when his self-award matches the teacher's assessment of his behavior. Token systems are designed to be faded. There are many different methods for fading reliance on tokens and for prolonging your child's ability to delay the receipt of a reward.

Problem Solving

A fourth strategy to assist children with autism in following rules is using a problem-solving instructional format. As shown in Table 3-11, the concept behind social problem solving training is to help children with autism identify the central problem in a situation, generate alternative courses of action to address the problem, anticipate the consequences of various courses of action, make a choice among the options, and evaluate the choice in light of the outcome (Shure, 1992).

Solving social problems (e.g., what to do when a peer treats you unfairly, how to join a game) is a challenge for most chil-

---

Table 3-11 | Stages of Problem Solving

1. Problem Identification
- identifying the central issue

2. Generation of Alternatives
- listing possible courses of action in the situation (at least 3 or 4)
- including positive and negative solutions

3. Anticipating Consequences
- guessing the likely effects of each course of action
- should include social consequences (e.g., how others will feel)

4. Making a Choice
- choosing the best alternative

5. Evaluating the Decision
- evaluating the effects of the choice
- learning from mistakes

dren with autism. They may have trouble identifying the central issue in social contexts. They may also find it hard to delineate a course of action and often appear to respond impulsively, with little forethought or reflection. It may be a novel experience for them to list multiple possible responses to a particular event. While listing the possible responses is a challenge, anticipating the results may bring even more difficulty. Perspective-taking skills, in which the child learns to consider the point of view of other people, are integral to this stage of the problem-solving process (see Chapter 4).

It may seem daunting to help your child understand others' reactions and the resulting social consequences, but developing this judgment will equip him with skills to make appropriate choices and assess the outcome of his choices. Learning to evaluate choices enables children to correct errors in similar situations in the future. Table 3-12 gives some examples of problem-solving strategies for children with autism.

Recognizing Correct Behavior

Another vital skill for social success is recognizing behaviors that are appropriate and inappropriate in a given context. Being able to do this helps your child recognize how others may perceive his behavior, and highlights the salient aspects of behavior. Two methods that can help many children achieve this understanding are role play and video instruction.

Role Play

Role plays, in which one or more individuals acts out a particular situation, can be used in a variety of ways. As shown in Table 3-13 on page 94, the actors can include puppets or doll characters, or they can include actual people. They can also involve the child with autism as a participant in the role play.

At first, it is helpful for your child with autism to watch, rather than participate in, role plays. This way, his only task is to observe and understand the information presented in the role

Table 3-12 | Sample Problem-Solving Task

Lauren is on the playground. She is playing with a ball. Joey comes up to her and grabs the ball away. Lauren pulls Joey's hair. The teacher comes over to see what is happening.

Problem Identification
Q: What is the problem?
A: Joey takes the ball without asking.

Generating Solutions
Q: What could Lauren do?
A1: Give the ball to Joey.
A2: Ask Joey to give it back.
A3: Pull Joey's hair.
A4: Hit Joey.
A5: Tell the teacher.

Potential Outcomes
Q: What might happen with each of these choices?
A1: Lauren feels sad, cries.
A2: Joey keeps the ball.
A3: Joey cries and tells the teacher, "Lauren pulled my hair." Lauren (& Joey) get in trouble.
A4: Joey cries and tells the teacher, "Lauren hit me." Lauren (& Joey) get in trouble.
A5: The teacher makes Joey give the ball back.

play. Being a participant significantly increases the demands to attend and generate responses, and some children may be overwhelmed with these simultaneous demands.

Using doll characters and puppets simplifies the planning for these instructional sessions, so our examples will focus on doll characters and puppets. However, using these toys makes it harder for children with autism to generalize the information to another situation, and should not be the sole method of role play

---

Table 3-13 | Variations of Role Plays for Two Main Players

- Two doll characters
- Two puppets
- Two instructors
- Instructor and another (typically developing) child
- Instructor and child with autism
- Two other children
- Child with autism and another child

---

instruction. It is essential that people become the players so that your child learns to apply the information in contexts similar to his actual experience.

Role-play scenarios can range from simple and brief to quite complex. A simple use of role play is to work on components of social interaction. Your child can learn to identify the presence or absence of specific social behaviors such as making eye contact or facing his partner within a role-play scenario. Table 3-14 lists examples of discrete social skills that can be targeted in this way.

Table 3-14 | Simple Role-Play Scenarios

- Facing a conversational partner
- Creating and maintaining appropriate physical distance
- Making eye contact with a conversational partner
- Looking at a partner when greeted
- Looking at someone when he enters the room
- Appropriate behavior while socially engaged (e.g., absence of self-stimulatory behavior)
- Answering questions posed by a conversational partner (vs. ignoring)
- Answering the question asked or making appropriate comments, rather than responding with irrelevant or nonsensical information.

Role-play scenarios can also be used to emphasize more complex or abstract social behaviors. Elaborate scenes of longer duration can target social difficulties such as reading the cues (body language) of a conversational partner, speaking about topics of interest to the other person, and providing the appropriate level of detail in response to questions

The role plays your child observes should include many examples of appropriate social behavior and much fewer examples of inappropriate behavior. As a rule of thumb, we suggest showing your child five correct models for every error. After the scene is played out, whether or not it contained an error, you can ask your child, using language appropriate to him, to discuss the scene. This can be as simple as asking, "Was that okay?" Or it can be as complicated as asking what things the person did well while he talked with his friend, and what things needed improvement.

Your child should then participate in correcting mistakes. You might discuss with him what could have been done better or differently. You could have him watch the same scenario again and then ask him whether the second enactment was better, and why. Typically, your re-enactment should correct the error. However, you can occasionally repeat the error to ensure that your child is truly paying attention to the role play. In other words, your child should not always expect the second "take" to be flawless because this may lead to patterned responding on his part. Alternately, your child can take the puppet and show you the correct behavior. It is important to know whether your child can handle this responsibility, or whether he becomes distracted by the task. While participating in the corrected sequence will be a very valuable learning experience, you must ensure that he has the prerequisite skills to benefit from this experience.

After your child shows an understanding of role plays with dolls or puppets, you can use live actors. Again, it is usually helpful for your child to start by being an observer, not an actor, except possibly in the correction sequence, as noted above. When your child is eventually involved in acting out a role, it is wise to limit this role to appropriate behavior. (There is no need to have your child practicing inappropriate behaviors!)

Video Instruction

Video instruction is a powerful but underutilized teaching method for children with autism. It is well documented that many children with autism have strong visual skills, and it makes sense to use these strengths for teaching the most elusive of concepts. Both role play and video have the distinct advantage of providing information in a visual context.

Video segments, like role plays, can be used to teach a range of social behavior, from simple, discrete skills to more complex interactions. In addition, video segments make possible some teaching that would be difficult with role plays. Videos provide an excellent forum for modeling appropriate behavior. For example, it may be possible to videotape circle times at school. Your child can then watch peers engaging in appropriate behavior. It may be particularly helpful to tape a specific child. Your child could then sit near this "good model" during the actual circle times.

Some parents have used these tapes not only to identify appropriate behavior, but also to get their children to practice it. Your child could watch the video as if it were circle time, and participate accordingly. This is a creative way to get many more opportunities to practice circle time behavior. It also has added generalization advantages because it is a video of the actual teacher and setting in which the behavior will be required.

While it may be tempting to also videotape the inappropriate behaviors of peers, this is usually not as helpful. We want to emphasize the appropriate behaviors, and encourage emulation of these skills.

Videotaping your own child can be an excellent way to provide very specific feedback to him on his social behavior. Most importantly, it can be used to provide reinforcement to him for all of the behaviors he is doing well. When watching the video, you can pause and provide specific praise for jobs well done! It can also be useful in highlighting skills that need to be improved.

You can, for example, videotape your child in a mock circle time with several neighborhood children. You can then watch this tape with your child to identify all the things he is doing well, as well as to identify areas for improvement. Table 3-15 describes one such use of videotape to teach a child the rules of circle time.

Table 3-15 | Sam Learns about Circle Time

Sam worked with his sister and a friend in a mock circle time as part of his home program. His instructor did a ten-minute circle time. She led them in a greetings song and activity, she read a story and asked questions, she did the calendar, and she led them in two participatory songs. On the video, Sam was listening to the teacher, looking at his friends, doing the actions to the songs, raising his hand, and waiting his turn. Sam also, however, periodically stood up or stared at his hands.

Videos provide excellent opportunities for reinforcement. As you read the notes about Sam, look at all the things he was doing well. Watching the video with a child can be an immensely rewarding experience for everyone. Videos can also serve to educate the educators. In other words, you may see things on the video that are worthy of attention. In the example above, Sam will likely be more successful in school if he can stay seated at circle and if his hand staring becomes less frequent.

We have found that using videos is extremely successful with children with autism. Often, children who have been struggling with a particular goal are much more successful after they have watched it on video. Videos are also excellent bridges into self-assessment and self-monitoring (in which your child monitors and evaluates his own behavior). As children become more aware of their behavior, they become much better evaluators of their performance. This can have tremendous implications for behavior management.

We do urge caution in using videos to identify instructional targets (i.e., skill deficits that need to be addressed). It is important to ensure that viewing the videos does not become an aversive experience for your child. The vast majority of your comments should be positive, and should focus on things being done well. If you do use videos to address social skill lapses, it should only be for well-mastered skills that your child has not demonstrated in this particular instance. Corrective comments should represent only a tiny fraction of the comments made while watching the tape. In addition, it may be best to simply ask in this context, "What could you remember to do next time?"

One final caution: It is important to work closely with school personnel to ensure that you are following their regulations for videotaping. It may be necessary, for example, to get the permission of other parents, the principal, or the school board.

Getting and Giving Information

Getting and giving information are important aspects of functioning in a social environment. Children with autism tend neither to view others as sources of information nor to understand the importance of sharing information with someone else. This will impede their social activity, especially in school.

For our purposes, giving information requires that your child provide information to another person at her request. (See also our section below on "Social Initiations" for situations where information is given spontaneously.) Although your child may have learned to answer simple social questions such as "How old are you?" or "Where is the ball?," he also needs to follow the direction to give this information to another person. For example, he should be able to follow a teacher's instruction to "Tell her where the ball is" or follow his mother's request to "Tell your sister where the keys are." This kind of information sharing goes a step beyond merely providing the answer to a question.

Asking for information is especially important for children with autism because they often need assistance in following instructions. The best way to get that help is to ask the right questions. In addition, asking questions opens the door to more interactions, and provides a means of continuing a conversational exchange. Some of the instructions you can use to help your child learn to ask questions of others would be, "Ask mommy what she had for breakfast," "Ask your sister where the crayons are," and "Ask someone to help you." Table 3-16 lists a number of instructions to prompt children to ask questions.

Table 3-16 | Sample Prompts to Encourage Children to Ask Questions

- Ask Mommy her favorite dessert.
- Ask Daddy where he works.
- Ask Joey where the crayons are.
- Ask someone to help you.
- Ask for help in opening the jar.
- Ask Millie what she wants to eat.
- Ask Jessica what color she needs.
- Ask Mrs. Smith how to get to the cafeteria (assuming skills to get teacher attention are established).
- Ask Mr. Robbins where the bathroom is (assuming skills to get teacher attention are established).

Ideally, your child should eventually be able to ask questions without the scripting in Table 3-16. The goal is for him to generalize these skills to naturally occurring situations where they will have meaning in his life. One way to accomplish this generalization is to create analog situations (artificial situations that mimic real ones) that allow your child to rehearse, under your guidance, situations he will later encounter outside of the house. For example, you could send your child to ask a neighbor for a cooking ingredient, to ask a police officer for directions, or to ask a store clerk where an item is.

If your child needs prompts in analog training, nonverbal prompts—such as cards with written cues—are preferable, as they promote independence and are easier to fade. It is also best if a second instructor provides the prompts. This way, the main instructor does not become embedded in the task, and your child does not become dependent on the assistance of his primary instructor. If your child does not respond to any other instructor, it would be best to address that difficulty in generalization first. Because problems in generalizing will affect progress in all areas, you should make sure your child is able to respond to more than one instructor in the early stages of ABA programming. Some suggestions on generalization strategies can be found in two books listed at the end of this chapter: *Behavioral Intervention for Young Children with Autism* and *Right from the Start.*

Maintaining a Conversation

While many children with autism become adept at answering simple questions and providing social information, few master the art of "conversational persistence"—that is, the ability to keep a conversation going back and forth between participants. Instead, they tend to have fleeting conversations, which largely consist of responding to the questions of others. As we describe below, to develop social relationships, your child will need to learn to initiate, to comment, and to sustain interactions.

Social Initiations

Social initiation involves approaching others to interact or to join an ongoing activity. There are several reasons to target social initiations in children with autism (Nelson & Wright, 2000). The most important of these is that children with autism seldom make social initiations without specific instruction. Social initiation skills open doors for social relationships with peers and are especially important in school. Equipping children with autism with these skills will empower them to succeed in social environments and will reduce their dependency on adults to orchestrate interactions with peers.

Several types of social initiations may have special relevance for classroom involvement. It will be important for your child to

be able to initiate to (i.e., approach) peers, to build links with others, and to stay tuned in to what is going on, rather than isolating himself. It will also be important for your child to initiate interactions with his teacher, particularly when he is having trouble with class work.

Initiating or Joining an Activity. One type of initiation is to approach someone to begin a social activity. For example, a child may ask his father to sing or read with him, or ask his sister to play with a specific toy. A child with limited verbal skills might use picture symbols or written words to invite another child to play.

Another type of initiation is to ask permission to join an activity that is in progress. A child can learn to ask, "Can I play?" This skill is appropriate to teach once your child has mastered turn taking, can wait briefly, and can stay on task for three to five minutes. It is often first addressed in an analog format. An instructor and another child may be playing a game. A second instructor would prompt the child with autism to request to join the activity. Initially, the child would always be allowed to join. Over time, the variety of games, activities, and people involved would increase. In addition, the child's request would occasionally be refused. This gradually prepares him for the diversity of possibilities likely to be encountered in daily experience.

Asking What Another Person Is Doing. One type of initiation that may be especially helpful for enhancing social connections is to ask others about their activities. Your child should learn to inquire about what other children are drawing, building, making, etc. For example, your child can ask another child, "What are you building?"

As with other skills, this would first be taught in an analog setting, and would usually include the use of a second instructor. Generalization of this skill would be systematically addressed, until your child was able to demonstrate the skill with his peers. Most children will respond to these questions and may be flattered by the attention. This can lead into a request to join in either a parallel or cooperative play situation.

Help Me, Please. An initiation that is extremely important for classroom functioning and to success in an inclusive classroom is asking the teacher or a peer for help. Fortunately, several strategies can be used to teach children with autism to say they need information (Taylor and Harris, 1995).

When your child does not know how to answer a question or to do a task, an important first step is for him to recognize that he doesn't know the information. That is, he needs to be able to say, "I don't know." Only then can he ask for the information he needs. While it is often possible to teach "I don't know" in a variety of question and answer formats, it may be helpful to expand this skill using additional formats.

To create opportunities for learning to say, "I don't know," identify a group of known items and a group of unknown items. Your child should already have learned to label a group of known objects such as car, truck, and book. An unknown item can be inserted into this chain of known items, and your child can learn to say, "I don't know" for the novel item. This skill can be expanded to include a request for the information (e.g., "I don't know. What is it?") This skill can also be taught to nonverbal children using an augmentative communication system. Your child's picture communication system or voice output device could be programmed to include a response for "I don't know" and "What is it?"

Table 3-17 provides an example of a program for teaching a child to say "I don't know."

Table 3-17 | Teaching "I Don't Know"

1. Instructor lays out three known items (car, truck, and book) and asks, "What are these?"
2. Child labels chain of items (Car, truck, book)
3. Instructor provides reinforcement.
4. Instructor lays out two known items and one unknown item (car, screwdriver, truck).
5. Child says "car." At screwdriver, child says, "I don't know. What is it?"
6. Instructor labels "screwdriver."
7. Child completes chain, labeling "truck."
8. Instructor provides reinforcement.

Note: For step 5, child will initially be prompted to indicate the response. A second instructor may verbally prompt the child to say the words or to give a picture of the object to the instructor. Sometimes after children have learned how to say, "I don't know, what is it?" they may make guesses rather than ask for help. Guessing may be handled differently depending on the child. A guess that is a close guess should be reinforced. A child who guesses rather automatically, however, and whose guesses are random might instead be prompted to give the "I don't know" response.

After your child has learned a label for an unknown item, it becomes a known one and is replaced with other novel items. Also be sure that unknown items are placed randomly in the beginning, middle, and end of the sequence of items.

Another way to increase requests for help from teachers and others is to create situations in which your child is motivated to ask for help. Start with activities that are very motivating such as help in opening a juice box or a container of candy. It is important to prompt your child to request assistance before severe frustration occurs. It is often helpful to have a second instructor prompt your child to ask for assistance. This will ensure rapid fading (systematic reduction) of prompts and will maximize independence.

Commenting

One of the ways in which typically developing children sustain an interaction is through the comments they make to their peers. They notice things and events in the environment, they narrate what others do, and they invite others into their experience. Although children with autism often become adept at answering questions and may develop skills in initiating conversations, these interactions are often quite fleeting. Adding the skills of commentary to their repertoire will help them to sustain their interactions with their peers.

There are several types of commenting/sharing, including joint attention, noticing others' works, noticing environmental objects, and commenting on the play of others.

Joint Attention. As we noted earlier, joint attention is a social skill that develops in infancy. A baby will look to his parent when he discovers that a rattle shakes. While he doesn't yet have the words to say, "Look at this," he says it with his eyes. This ability becomes more developed and more complex as his language ability improves. Children draw the attention of others to things they are doing, things they see, toys they are exploring, and abilities they discover. These are the ways that children share their experiences and include others in their developmental discoveries.

Joint attention is almost always absent in children with autism and nearly always requires systematic instruction. The most basic form of joint attention may be simply to request that others look at something. One way to teach this is through the use of a "surprise bag" that contains unusual and visually interesting items. You can introduce this activity by first opening a surprise bag yourself and showing your child the contents. This way, he learns that surprises in the bag can be interesting. Your child can be taught to solicit your attention before *he* opens the bag, by tapping your shoulder or by saying something like, "Look at this!" Next, to work with your child on responding to the joint attention overtures of others, switch roles. That is, you bring out the surprise bag, and get your child's attention before opening it. This task serves to build commenting skills and to establish a form of joint attention.

Another important commenting task is to notice the work of others. Children often compliment each other during school activities. At the very least, they often acknowledge what other children are doing. Your child can learn to take notice of the work and products of other children, and to comment on them. Initially, you might model such comments for your child, by pointing out both his work and the work of others. You may have to target this skill more systematically, however, and you may need to script such social overtures for your child. Some of the many opportunities for such commentary are listed in Table 3-18.

Table 3-18 | Opportunities for Commentary

- Art projects ("I like your picture.")
- Drawings ("That's a pretty flower.")
- Paintings ("I like the red car.")
- Sand creations ("Cool colors!")
- Block creations ("That's a big tower.")
- Lego creations ("That's a tall castle.")

For some children, teaching them to involve others can take a creative step beyond the programs we have already described. In the box on the next page is a description of how one child's parents used events that were especially unusual to help their son share more things with other people. They used the technology of ABA, and applied it creatively to their son's individual way of learning.

Do You See What I See?

Neil was progressing nicely through both language and social skills programs. He had even done well in learning how to initiate interactions with other children and to join group activities. His teacher commented, though, that she didn't really ever see Neil try to get the attention of others the way her other students did. He never showed friends something he had or something he was working on or making. She thought this limited the amount and types of interactions he had with peers.

Neil had been through all of the "programs" in this regard. We had used the surprise bag, and we had focused on noticing the work of others. While he had mastered these skills, they had not evolved into more naturalistic interactions. One thing that Neil's parents noted was that he did get people's attention when very unusual events happened at home. They remembered that once when a candle from a birthday cake fell onto the table, and sparked a flame, Neil had said, "Hey, everyone, the table's on fire." He also noted more mundane, unexpected events. For example, if a balloon popped, or a toy fell off a shelf, or a door flew open, he would notice *and* he would attempt to share the event with others. Neil's parents and behavior analyst brainstormed about how to use this strength to build skills in this area.

Neil's parents began surprising Neil in a variety of ways. For example, his mother might put Neil's favorite video in his backpack or a big box of candy in his lunchbox. Once, Neil's Dad came to visit the class. These unexpected and highly reinforcing events always sparked an attempt on Neil's part to gain the attention of others, to share the experience. Over time, the surprises became more ordinary. For example, Neil might find a baseball card or a photo of his dog in his lunchbox. He shared these events as well.

A special form of commenting, play narration, was discussed in Chapter Two. The instructional sequence described there builds elaborate and sustained commenting skills. That skill is helpful for building cooperative play with peers, and represents a more thematic and sustained form of commenting. The skill can also be extended into noticing other environmental objects, such as new books or interesting toys. When children make comments to others, others usually reply and may ask follow-up questions or otherwise prolong the interaction.

The commenting skills described above are simple and fairly limited. Nevertheless, their inclusion in your child's program will equip him with additional skills to interact with others. These skills will also help others see your child as an interactive partner and as an observant and vibrant member of the classroom.

Sustaining Interactions

To help children sustain a conversation, we focus on developing skills in reciprocity—that is, in keeping the conversational "ball" going back and forth. Being skilled in reciprocal conversation enables a child to hold a sustained conversation with another person.

Responding with Similar Information. One fundamental skill in reciprocal interaction is to offer similar information when someone offers you information. For example, a child learns to give his name when another person introduces himself. This type of reciprocal interaction can easily be taught with information mastered in a Social Questions program. A Social Questions program is something that children in ABA programs typically master in the earlier stages of programming. In this program, a child learns to answer questions about his name, age, likes, and dislikes. (Sample questions in a Social Questions program include "What's your name?," "What's your favorite food?," "Who is your favorite Pokeman character?" etc.)

This concept can then be extended to a reciprocal play format, with characters or animals. Table 3-19 on the next page has examples of reciprocal exchanges that might be done with hand puppets and Table 3-20, also on the next page, shows some exchanges for role plays of community helpers. Initially, the instructor would lead these interactions, and your child would be prompted as needed, with a specific question (e.g., "What is your name?")

One important element of reciprocity is increasing the number of reciprocal exchanges, or back-and-forth conversational turns. A single exchange is complete when both individuals have

Table 3-19	Reciprocal Exchange: Puppets or Dolls	
My name is Rags.	My name is Kitty.
I am a dog.	I am a cat.
I say woof woof.	I say meow.
I like to take walks.	I like to lie in the sun.
I lick when I'm happy.	I purr when I'm happy.

Table 3-20	Reciprocal Exchange: Community Helpers	
I am a firefighter.	I am a police officer.
I put out fires.	I help people.
I work in the firehouse.	I work in the police station.
I drive a fire truck.	I drive a police car.

spoken once. At first, the goal will be for your child to complete one exchange. He will simply reciprocate when a conversational partner makes a statement, and receive a reward at the end of his exchange. Over time, however, your child will be expected to take multiple turns to lengthen the interaction and add to the complexity of the conversation. You will then reinforce him for making the targeted number of exchanges.

Joining in Others' Conversations. Another type of conversational participation involves more than one conversational partner. Children can be taught to listen to the conversations of others, and then to join in those conversations appropriately. Listening skills are centrally important.

Often, children with autism pay no attention to conversations when they are not involved. To help your child tune in to others' conversations, you can use an analog format, in which your child listens to a staged conversation between two instructors. At first, the conversation may be only one or two exchanges. Your child would then be asked, "What did Sally say?" or "What are they talking about?" Over time, your child would be prompted to join the conversation in an appropriate way. It may be helpful to have your child initially listen to a conversation about something that interests him. However, it is important that the skill be extended beyond areas of personal interest.

Asking Questions. Reciprocal conversation has limits as a means of sustaining a conversation. After all, it only teaches your child to respond with information similar to what someone else says. These types of exchanges are useful and appropriate, especially for pretend play, but children need to learn other ways to prolong interactions.

One way to sustain a conversation is to ask questions about someone else's preferences, desires, and experiences. A good strategy for introducing question asking is to build on reciprocal conversation skills by teaching your child to add a related question to his response. For example, if the first child says, "I like pizza," the second child might say, "Me too. Do you like French fries?"

An instructional tool that can be helpful in building conversational skills is *Comic Strip Conversations* (Gray, 1994). This method, developed by Carol Gray, provides children with a visual record of a spoken interaction. It is designed to increase clarity in conversation. In these comic strips, each conversational exchange is depicted with a cartoon-like drawing, and multiple interactions (i.e., exchanges) can fit on a single page. A Comic Strip Conversation can be about any topic, and can be as simple as exchanging greetings. (See the example on the next page.) Once a Comic Strip Conversation has been created, the instructor and child can practice by reading the parts. This tool is helpful for children who have difficulties following conversations and coming up with the right things to say. It can also be helpful for generalizing conversational skills.

Comic Strip Conversations can be used to teach other elements of communication, too, including types of communication such as questions or exclamations, and emotional elements such as anger. The highly visual nature of the materials appeals to and matches the strengths of many children with autism. Remember, however, that the research basis of this method of teaching is still very limited.

For more information on teaching your child conversational skills, you may wish to read *The Me Book* by psychologist Ivar Lovaas (1981). Lovaas created the most comprehensive programs for developing conversational skills in children with autism, and his work on reciprocal conversation has helped others develop methods to address this difficulty. Two of his former students, Ron Leaf and John McEachin, have summarized much of Lovaas's work in this area of curricular development in their book, *A Work in Progress* (1999). Additional information on social language programming can be found in *Behavioral Intervention for Young Children with Autism,* by Catherine Maurice and her colleagues (1996).

Slang, Idioms, & Expressions

One day, Joey was sitting with his friends at snack. He was enjoying the cookies, as were his companions. The teacher saw Joey's eager expression and looked into the bag of cookies. She said, "Joey, there's a cookie in here with your name on it." Joey reached for the bag, looked at the cookies, and became upset. "There's no cookie with my name on it. There's no cookie that says Joey." He stormed away. His classmates snickered and whispered.

Like many children with autism, Joey was unable to understand and use the slang, idioms, and expressions of his peer group. Understanding idioms and the figurative use of language requires that a child recognize that words are not always literal in meaning. Helping your child to understand this concept will assist him in social situations when they are used.

In this program, your child is introduced to the slang and figurative expressions most commonly used in his culture. As shown in Table 3-21 on the next page, there are countless examples that you can use. The instructor might say, "Sometimes people say that it's raining cats and dogs. Is it really raining cats and dogs?" When your child answers, "No," the adult asks, "What does 'it's raining cats and dogs' really mean?" Your child might then say, "It is raining really hard." The reasoning behind such expressions can be explained to varying extents, depending upon your child's language abilities. For example, you might say "Raining cats and dogs" means it is raining so hard it is like the drops are as big as cats and dogs!"

Table 3-21 | Common Expressions & Their Meaning

I'm so hungry I could eat a horse. .... I am VERY hungry.

It's raining cats and dogs. .... It's raining very hard.

You're pulling my leg. .... You're teasing/kidding me.

He/she laughed his/her head off. .... He laughed a lot, for a long time, etc.

Running around like a chicken .... Running in circles, confused.
with its head cut off.

Don't bug me. .... Leave me alone, stop bothering me.

Break a leg. .... Do a good job. Good luck.

Like a fish out of water. .... Uncomfortable, not fitting in.

You can't judge a book by its cover. .... You can't tell what a person is like from how he/she looks.

He/she knows me like a book. .... He/she knows me very well.

He/she is dancing around the question. .... He/she isn't answering directly.

His eyes were popping out of his head. ..... He was surprised.

He is growing like a weed. .... He is growing fast.

Keep your eye out. .... Watch carefully.

Reach for the stars. .... Try very hard; expect the best.

Buzz off. .... Leave me alone.

Shake a leg. .... Hurry up.

Butt out. .... Mind your own business.

Pipe down. .... Quiet down.

Chill out. .... Relax.

Hanging out. .... Relaxing, spending time together.

Scaredy cat. .... Afraid (usually mean).

It's apples and oranges. .... It's two different things.

A watched pot never boils. .... It's hard to wait; it seems even longer when you think about it.

I see the light. .... I understand.

The early bird catches the worm. .... The earliest person gets the best choice.

The squeaky wheel gets the grease. .... Talking (complaining) gets results.

A bird in hand is worth two in the bush. ... It's better to have something than to hope for something better.

Let sleeping dogs lie. .... Forget about it.

Telling Jokes

Childhood is full of humor. However, telling and appreciating jokes can be challenging for children with autism because you need to understand silliness and punning to be effective at joking. Joking is an important means of connecting with peers, and children with autism sometimes have difficulty managing this social challenge.

One of the first steps to developing skills in this area is to be able to identify what is missing from or wrong with a particular situation or picture. Table 3-22 has lists of absurd or incongruent

---

Table 3-22 | The Inconsistent, Illogical, and Absurd

What's missing (items with missing parts)?
- Car without wheels
- Boat without sail
- House without roof
- Person without shoe
- Face without eyes, nose, mouth, etc.

Misplaced items
- Person with hat on foot
- Person with shoe on head
- Car with sail
- Car with square wheel
- Roof beneath the rest of house

Illogical items
- Eating with a pencil
- Brushing hair with a spoon
- Cutting with a fork
- Wearing shorts in the snow
- Wearing sunglasses in the rain

Absurd items
- A dog on roller blades
- A person walking on water
- A cat using a spoon
- A baby driving a car
- A boy sleeping in a dog bed

items that can be taught to lay the groundwork for humor. These progress from items that are simply wrong to those that are ridiculous. When you are first showing your child silly pictures, you might smile and giggle to indicate that it is silly. You might also label such things as silly, wrong, or ridiculous.

Once your child can identify what is wrong in a variety of pictures, he is probably ready for simple jokes. His attempts at joking are very likely to sound like the attempts of very young children described in the introduction to this chapter. He may announce that he is telling a joke, and then say something that may or may not be amusing. He may say sounds or words that he expects to be perceived as funny. You may want to laugh at these early attempts, simply to encourage your child's attempts at humor. Since he has been exposed to information on absurdities, however, he will have some ideas of potentially funny material and may repeat items from those programs.

The knock-knock jokes of childhood are a logical next step in learning about humor. Many children with autism need systematic instruction in this area as well. In other words, it can be helpful to take your child through the joke step by step, and explain why and where it is funny. For some children, looking at a written joke helps them understand the humor. Plays on words, for example, may be seen more readily in written format. Table 3-23 has several of the classic jokes of this genre.

Before teaching your child to tell and understand a knock-knock joke, make sure he already knows that "knock-knock" is responded to with "who's there?" It may be helpful when teaching this skill to have a second instructor assisting your child with his responses. It may help to write out all of the lines of the joke. This can provide your child with a textual prompt, and may also help him understand some of the "funny" elements of the joke. For example, in the advanced example, the instructor can point out that "orange" sounds like "aren't you." The instructor can also point out that an orange is also a fruit, so it makes sense after banana.

Once your child has the sense of knock-knock jokes, you can fade out the scripting and the visual supports. It is impor-

Table 3-23 | Telling a Knock-Knock Joke

Beginner

Instructor: Knock-knock.
Child: Who's there?
Instructor: Hatch.
Child: Hatch who?
Instructor: Bless you.

Instructor: Knock-knock
Child: Who's there?
Instructor: Boo.
Child: Boo who?
Instructor: What happened? Why are you crying?

Instructor: Knock-knock.
Child: Who's there?
Instructor: Harry.
Child: Harry who?
Instructor: Harry up and answer the door.

Advanced

Instructor: Knock-knock.
Child: Who's there?
Instructor: Banana.
Child: Banana who?
Instructor: Knock-knock.
Child: Who's there?
Instructor: Banana.
Child: Banana who?
Instructor: Knock-knock.
Child: Who's there?
Instructor: Orange.
Child: Orange who?
Instructor: Orange you glad I didn't say banana?

tant to ensure that your child has been exposed to enough of these jokes that he responds to naturally encountered knock-knock jokes appropriately.

Other types of jokes can be introduced in a similar manner, being sure to provide sufficient explanations and examples of each type of humor. It may also be helpful to teach your child to watch how others react to humor. If he has difficulty recognizing humor, he can learn to rely on peers' reactions and tone of voice to determine whether something is meant to be a joke.

Using Gestures

Social language consists of gestures and expressions as well as words. Nonverbal communication happens all the time, in all our interactions. One of the ways we evaluate how another person is reacting to what we say is to tune into his nonverbal behaviors. Is the person looking at me? Is he distracted? Is he fidgeting? We alter our own behavior in response to what we see.

Children, too, learn to monitor nonverbal behavior at an early age. They learn, for example, what signs mean that someone is interested or not interested in what they are saying, and they modify their behavior in response to these cues. There are four essential steps in this process: 1) recognizing nonverbal communication, 2) understanding it, 3) responding to it, and 4) using the information gained in a nonverbal communication.

Children with autism have difficulty with this process because they must perceive and interpret other people's subtle actions and adjust their own behavior according to what they learn. There are a great many nonverbal gestures to be learned by the child with autism (Table 3-24).

Table 3-24 | Common Nonverbal Communications
◆ Nodding yes
◆ Shaking head no
◆ Quiet (finger to mouth)
◆ Bad (shaking finger)
◆ Blowing a kiss
◆ Clapping for a job well done
◆ Waving
◆ Holding arms out (to be picked up)
◆ Putting out hand (for "give me")
◆ Shrugging shoulders (I don't know)
◆ Come here/Hurry up
◆ I want that (e.g., reaching for an item)
◆ I don't want that (e.g., handing an item back)
◆ I'm interested (looking, paying attention)
◆ I'm not interested (not looking, fidgeting, etc.)

Before working on these gestures with your child, make sure he has thoroughly mastered general compliance skills. Your child must absolutely possess the skills to follow directions before embarking on this program.

The first step in teaching the use of nonverbal communication strategies is to ensure that your child can recognize the basic nonverbal communications. For example, you would ask him to "Show me what this means," followed by a gesture such as "come here" or "quiet." He would be expected to come in response to a beckoning gesture or be silent in response to a finger to the lips.

Next, you would teach your child to imitate each of these actions, and to do them on request. For example, you would say to him, "Show me come here" and he would be expected to beckon with his hand. It is imperative that your child learns to use these gestures in real life, where they make sense. Take advantage of opportunities during your daily routine to use the gestures and help your child recognize what you have communicated. This incidental teaching will ensure that your child uses and interprets gestures in the social context where they are appropriate.

You can also work on nonverbal communication with your child in a story format, using story books, videos, or role plays. In the story format, you would show or tell your child a short story and then ask him how he could convey a particular message in that story without words. For example, how would he show that he wants help with a toy? It may be easier to let your child give you the words first. You can then ask him whether there is an-

---

Table 3-25 | Sequence of Programs for Teaching Nonverbal Communication

1. Receptive Identification
Present an array of photos (perhaps cut out of magazines) or picture symbols (drawings).
Say to child: "Touch 'go away'"

2. Expressive Identification
Demonstrate a gesture.
Say to child: "What does this mean?"

3. Imitation
Say to Child: "Do this" (demonstrating a gesture)

4. Engaging on request
Say to child: "Show me 'come here.'"

5. Stories
Tell child a story: "Joey gives Kayla a cookie. Kayla wants pretzels."
Ask child a question: "How can Kayla tell Joey that she doesn't want the cookie (without words)?"

6. Role Plays

other way to send the message or whether he can think of a way to do it without words. Table 3-25 summarizes the teaching steps involved in helping a child learn to interpret and use nonverbal social gestures.

In the role-play instructional format, your child watches enacted scenarios in which nonverbal communication is being used. You then ask him to identify the nonverbal communication or to show which gestures to use. For example, he can offer another toy to a peer who rejects the first one he is offered. He can retreat when told to go away. He can respond appropriately when told "no."

Your child can observe two people or two dolls or puppets interacting, or he can be one of the players. You can also use videotaped segments. As shown in Table 3-26, there are many variations of the role-play instructional format.

Table 3-26 | Vignettes for Role Play of
Nonverbal Gestures

Kevin wants to play with the Legos alone. Steve comes over and is begging to play with the Legos too. Kevin wants Steve to find something else to do. How can he tell him to go away (without words)?

All of the children are in the library. They are supposed to be quietly reading, but many are talking. The teacher wants to tell them to be quiet, but she doesn't want to disrupt the children who are quietly reading. What can she do?

Brian and Billy are outside on the playground. Billy keeps going over to Brian to play, but Brian keeps turning away from him. What message is Brian sending?

Alexis sees Sarah come home from daycare. She is excited to see her sister and to have someone to play with. How can she let her know that without saying a word?

Ensuring Comprehensive Understanding of Concepts

Many of the social skills discussed in this chapter are multi-element skills. In addition, they can be used quite differently in different contexts. Consequently, children with autism will need a lot of practice in rehearsing these skills. Remember, it is often helpful to teach them using multiple methods and multiple modalities (e.g., auditory, visual). It is also advisable to reinforce these concepts through the use of commercially available curricular materials and social games, which can be purchased through some of the resources listed in Appendix A. All of these materials are potentially relevant and will complement the teaching we have discussed in this chapter.

Summary

Social skills are a complex and vital area of curricular development for your child. It is important for your child to learn how to respond to, and initiate interactions with, other people. Developing conversational skills will ensure that your child can initiate and maintain conversations, and can inquire about others' experiences, needs, and interests. Social survival skills also include giving and getting information and using assertiveness skills. Your child will need to learn to manage his frustration appropriately, and to express his needs and feelings in socially appropriate ways. It will also be important for him to understand social rules and behavioral expectations regarding social behavior. Problem solving skills will help him to navigate the often-choppy waters of social interaction. Helping your child to understand nuances such as gestures, idioms and expressions, and jokes will markedly improve his comprehension of subtle communication. Using a variety of instructional methods and materials is recommended to ensure that your child is exposed to many different levels of learning and has a broad sense of how to apply his social skills.

References

Gray, C. (1994). *Comic strip conversations*. Arlington, TX: Future Horizons.

Gray, C. (1993). *The original social story book*. Arlington, TX: Future Horizons.

Gray, C. (1994). *The new social story book*. Arlington, TX: Future Education.

Harris, S. & Weiss, M.J. *Right from the start: Behavioral intervention for young children with autism*. Bethesda, MD: Woodbine House, 1998.

Leaf, R. & McEachin, J. (Eds.) (1999). *A work in progress: Behavior management strategies and a curriculum for intensive behavioral treatment of autism*. New York, NY: DRL Books.

Lovaas, O.I. (1981). *The Me Book: Teaching developmentally disabled children*. Austin, TX: Pro-Ed.

Maurice, C., Green, G. & Luce, S. C. (1996). *Behavioral intervention for young children with autism: A manual for parents and professionals*. Austin, TX: Pro-Ed.
(In particular, see the chapter by R. G. Romanczyk, "Behavior Analysis and Assessment: The Cornerstone to Effectiveness," pp. 195-217.)

Meiners, C. J. (2000). *Social Skills Books*. Laurel, MD: Patuxent Enterprises.

Nelson, N. M. & Wright, J. J. (2000, March). *Using activity schedules to promote social initiations by individuals with autism and related disorders*. Paper presented at COSAC conference, Atlantic City, NJ.

Shure, M. B. (1992). *I can problem solve*. Champaign, IL: Research Press.

Taylor, B. & Harris, S. L. (1995). Teaching children with autism to seek information. *Journal of Applied Behavior Analysis, 28,* 3-14.

Wojtowicz, K. (1996). *The barber shop*. Unpublished manuscript, Rutgers, The State University of New Jersey.

4 | Looking at Life from a Different Perspective

Scott Kimball Learns about His Sister's Distress

Five-year-old Rita fell off the backyard swing and scraped her knee. Blood dripping down her leg, she began to cry and wail "Mommy!" When Allison came out of the backdoor, she found Rita on the ground weeping. Scooping her up, she carried Rita inside, cleaned her knee, covered the scrape, and gave her some kisses. When the crisis had passed and Rita was happily at play again, Allison had time to think about what Scott did, or actually did not do, while Rita cried.

Scott had been playing in the sandbox when Rita fell. While Allison picked Rita up, Scott had stood by the swing set, looking at Rita, but not touching her or talking to her. Allison realized his behavior was an improvement from six months before, when he would have simply ig-nored Rita and continued to line up cars or walk in circles. He seemed to know that something was wrong, but he did not appear to have any idea how to behave toward his sister or even that he should call his mother for help. His seemingly indifferent reaction to Rita's pain would have to change if he was going to fit in with other children.

Fortunately, Matt Becker, their home programming consultant, had some ideas about helping Scott learn to express empathy. Matt agreed that Scott had become more observant of his sister since begin-ning the play programs, but he did not seem to know what to do if Rita got upset. The Kimballs were working on several programs to teach Scott to recognize other people's feelings. He could name feel-ings in photos and describe how a person might feel in different situ-ations. For example, when shown a set of pictures in which a boy is given some ice cream, he could say "happy" when asked, "How does the boy feel?" When shown another set of pictures in which a girl falls off her bicycle and hurts her arm, he could say "sad."

In addition to working on these formal teaching programs, Allison and Jack went out of their way to label feelings when they saw someone react with strong emotion. They were also giving Scott the names of feelings when he was happy, upset, angry, and so forth. The other day, Jack had been at the store with Scott when a boy about his age had a tantrum because he wanted candy. Jack knelt beside Scott and told him quietly, "That little boy is angry because he can't have the candy he wants. He feels very angry." Scott nodded soberly and then Jack asked him, "How does the boy feel?" Scott answered, "Angry." "Right, Scott, the boy feels angry," said Jack. When they got home from the store, Jack and Scott told Allison about the little boy. "How did the little boy feel?" asked Allison, and Scott answered, "Angry." "That's right, Scott, he felt angry because he could not have the candy."

Thanks to this teaching, Scott had labels for feelings and could usually describe what another person was feeling. He could also name his own emotions. What he could not do was understand how to react when someone else was experiencing a strong emotion.

Matt suggested that "Social Stories" (described in Chapter 3) might be a perfect way to introduce Scott to this kind of social problem solving. These stories are written specifically for the child who needs to learn a skill and they can be tailored exactly to the child's needs. Scott's first Social Story would be about what to do when Rita falls down and hurts herself. He could learn to pat her gently, say, "It's ok," and call his mother or father to come help. Jack and Allison would read the story with Scott. If Social Stories worked, they might try them for some of the other situations Scott would face as he began to spend a few hours each day in a regular preschool class.

How Do the Kimball Family Experiences Resemble Your Own?

Most families of children with autism tell us their child has problems understanding another person's point of view and showing empathy for her. Some children with autism seem to be indifferent to how people feel, while others recognize feelings but do not know how to respond to them. Some children may make tentative efforts to respond to another person's distress, but they lack a flexible repertoire to react to the nuances of the other person's needs.

Most of us learn how to console others and to share another person's joy without being systematically taught. We learn by watching the people around us and from the empathetic reactions our parents and others give us when we are experiencing an emotion. However, for children with autism, these skills are not an automatic part of their developmental progress. They need special help learning to recognize emotions and to respond to them.

Scott's ability to deal with others' feelings was typical of many children with autism in the early stages of treatment. Thanks to many hours of intensive ABA treatment, he had become increasingly aware of what other people were doing and he noticed their expressions of emotion, especially the more obvious ones, such as his sister's tears or her laughter. What he did not yet understand was how to respond to these expressions.

The teaching programs in this chapter describe ways to help your child with autism develop a greater awareness of other people. We offer ways to increase your child's ability to adopt another person's perspective and to understand how another child or adult might think or feel.

What Is Perspective Taking?

The term "perspective taking" refers to the capacity to understand an experience from another person's point of view. It is the ability to "stand in the shoes" of another individual. To do this, we have to be able to recognize that our own feelings may differ from other people's, and be able to distinguish our emotions from others'.

Some people have more "intuition" than others about what someone else feels or thinks, but most of us have developed fairly

good skills in recognizing how other people might view the world. Some professions such as salesperson, teacher, or psychotherapist require very high levels of skill in perspective taking to be successful. Being an effective parent also draws heavily on the ability to adopt the child's perspective. And to sustain friendships with others requires us to use utmost sensitivity in understanding what they are feeling and where they are coming from.

Perspective taking poses a particular challenge for people with autism and is a significant barrier to the development of intimate friendships. Indeed, adults with autism often express perplexity at trying to understand what the typical person means by "friendship." A relative lack of skill in perspective taking is one of the major challenges to the person with autism who wishes to move comfortably in the mainstream social world.

The teaching activities in this chapter focus on helping your child develop a more refined ability to take the perspective of another person. Some of these programs lay the groundwork by teaching fundamentals such as recognizing and labeling feelings, or understanding that if you are standing in front of the television and I am behind it, I cannot see the show you are watching. Other programs are more advanced and teach such skills as the ability to recognize dishonesty and to express compassion for other people.

What Is Theory of Mind?

You may have heard the term "theory of mind" in conjunction with autism. Theory of mind refers to the ability to recognize that other people have inner thoughts and feelings—that they have "minds" that are different and separate from one's own.

Research suggests that people with autism tend to assume that other people know the same things they know. For example, a child with autism who has a new child in her class may assume that her parents know that child's name and may not realize that she needs to tell them before they are aware of the new child. Children with autism who do not understand what is shared knowledge and what they alone know are unlikely to realize the importance of sharing their thoughts or experiences.

A vivid example of the impact of theory of mind deficits is shown in the research of the British psychologist Simon Baron-Cohen and his colleagues (1985). In their research, children with autism were shown two dolls. One doll, Sally, had a basket. The other doll, Ann, had a marble. After Ann put her marble in Sally's basket, she left the room. Sally, a mischievous little doll, took the marble out of the basket and put it in a box. Ann then returned to the room.

The question now posed to the children with autism was, "Where will Ann look for her marble?" Unlike the typically developing children, who knew that Ann would look in the basket where she last left the marble, the children with autism said she would look in the box. In other words, the children with autism did not grasp that Ann, because she was out of the room, could not see where Sally moved the marble. They attributed to Ann the knowledge that they had from their own observations of Sally, not understanding that Ann could not share the information. This task can be readily done by most typically developing four-year-old children, but many much older children with autism have a hard time with it.

Considerable research has been done on the concept of theory of mind. Much of that work is beyond the scope of our book and of interest primarily to developmental psychologists studying the details of theory of mind. What is important for our purposes is that the Sally-Ann research illustrates nicely a common problem shown by many, but not all children with autism. If you want to read more about theory of mind, see Francesca Happe's book, *Autism: An Introduction to Psychological Theory,* listed at the end of this chapter.

How Does Perspective Taking Typically Develop?

A baby recognizes changes in emotion on others' faces, especially her mother's face. She may respond to a shift in her mother's expression with a change in her own behavior. However, the infant does not yet realize that these expressions reflect an inner state on the part of her caretaker. A baby will not attempt to comfort a crying mother, nor reflect on her mother's state of mind.

A child with autism will similarly recognize some clear *affective* (i.e., emotional) states of her parents and may modify her behavior in response to these changes. If her father raises her voice and speaks sternly, the child with autism may cease an unwanted behavior. This may be especially true if a stern tone from father has sometimes been followed by consequences such as being put in time-out. What the girl may not realize is that this change in expression and loud voice reflect an inner state experienced by her father.

All very young children have been described as "egocentric." Essentially, children believe the world revolves around them. They may express the idea that the moon is following them, for example. This technical term also refers to the child's difficulty in understanding the difference between her point of view and that of another person. We see this difficulty in the two-year-old who plays "hide and seek" by closing her own eyes and assuming no one can see her.

However, children this young are not devoid of empathy and there are situations in which they show their understanding of another person's perspective. For example, they can typically recognize another child's distress and try to comfort that child. They may pat the other child or offer a favorite toy to console her. Offering this comfort reflects not only the perception that another child is crying, but also the capacity to take on the perspective of that child and realize her tears reflect her distress. In addition, children who observe another child's distress typically feel some distress themselves: I see you cry, know that you are upset, and I am moved to try to console you.

Perspective taking is not limited to the understanding of another person's feelings. As we mentioned earlier in this chapter, it also involves recognizing that one's own knowledge may not be the same as another person's. In this cognitive (intellectual) realm, a typical four-year-old child can understand, on a basic level, that if she stands on one side of an object and you on the other, you cannot see what she sees. At a more refined level of perspective taking, it is not until her teenage years that a child begins to understand that you and I may know the same facts, but interpret them very differently.

Preschool-aged children have difficulty grasping that a person can have private emotions that are not expressed. It is not until the age of six years or so that children understand that you can feel one thing and say another. For example, someone can say she is happy, but actually be quite sad. Also by the age of six or seven years, the typically developing child is increasingly aware of how her own perception differs from other people's. She realizes that her behavior has an impact on another person, and may stop what she is doing to avoid hurting someone else's feelings. This stands in contrast to the younger child, who often needs the help of a parent or other adult to refrain from an upsetting behavior.

As they get older, children form more sophisticated judgments of people. They recognize, for example, that one person is often sad and another usually very jovial. A girl may come to realize that her grandfather is usually cheerful and can be counted on to be good-natured, while her uncle is often in ill humor and must be approached with care. Our ability to adopt the perspective of others grows in richness as we mature.

Perspective Taking in People with Autism

Most of the research on the recognition of emotions and inner states by people with autism has been done with teenagers and adults. Catherine Lord points out that it is difficult to do research in this area, especially with young children whose speech and language is limited (1993). Work by R. Peter Hobson (1993) and his colleagues, however, suggests that the biggest challenges for people with autism are not related to labeling feelings in photos, but, rather, interpreting more complex emotions and inner states that cannot be depicted in a single photo.

Observations by both parents and professionals suggest that children with autism show less sensitivity and affection to other people and are less likely than other children to comfort another child. This diminished responsiveness may not be terribly obvious to parents, Lord notes, if for example, the parents are especially stimulating and active in engaging their child. These sensitive parenting behaviors tend to obscure the fact that it is the parents, not the child, who is initiating interactions. Lord also observes that children with autism smile less in response to others' smiles, make fewer efforts to share objects of interest with their parents, and are less emotionally expressive during play with their parents than are typically developing children.

In addition to having a less emotionally expressive relationship with their parents, research suggests that children with autism pay less attention to peers than do other children. Indifference to brothers and sisters is another behavior that often separates the child with autism from other youngsters.

In sum, there are considerable challenges facing the young child with autism in learning to understand the perspective of another person. Still, we have recently made considerable progress in helping many of these youngsters become more attuned to their peers, their parents, and other adults. The information in this chapter offers guidance in creating programs to help your child learn that other people have different perspectives on the world and that we respond to the needs other people revealed through their expressions, behaviors, and words.

As you begin this work, remember that one of the hardest things children with autism need to learn is how "to stand in the shoes" of other people. Adopting the point of view of others requires coordination among language skills, abstract thought, and social understanding, as well as a capacity to respond to others with compassion. These are areas that are a significant challenge, so perspective taking is likely to be an especially hard domain to master.

The key to making progress in teaching your child with autism to understand what other people are feeling and thinking is to "think small." Small increments of understanding may eventually enable your child to comprehend the "big picture." Not all children will develop the highest level of perspective taking skills, but most will master at least some of these skills. These skills may be easier for children who have little cognitive impairment than for children who have more substantial intellectual challenges.

Developing Perspective Taking Skills

Table 4-1 lists the prerequisite skills to teach before working on perspective taking. Under the heading of language skills, your

---

Table 4-1 | Prerequisite Skills for Perspective Taking

Language Skills
- ◆ Receptive and expressive identification of emotions
- ◆ Yes/No
- ◆ I/You discrimination
- ◆ "Wh" question discrimination (including why)
- ◆ Reciprocity

Social Skills
- ◆ Identification of emotions in simple stories
- ◆ Identification of emotions of others in context
- ◆ Identification of emotions of self in context
- ◆ Identification of multiple emotions in one person (self or other)
- ◆ Identification of multiple emotions for multiple individuals
- ◆ Social responses (e.g., saying "Bless you")
- ◆ Some awareness of real versus pretend

child needs to use the labels of emotions, both expressively and receptively. For example, in the vignette about Scott, we described how he learned to recognize the happy, sad, or angry feelings of other people. Your child should also be able to use "Yes" and "No" correctly, recognize the difference between "I" and "you," and answer "wh" questions such as "Where is the dog?" or "Who fell down?" In addition, she should be able to have a reciprocal conversation with another person about such basics as what she likes to do or her age. (If a particular child does not possess all of these skills, she may still be able to learn some, but not all, of the perspective taking skills discussed below.)

In addition to language skills, your child needs to demonstrate some fundamental social skills before learning perspective taking. For example, she should be able to describe how a child in a story would feel if she fell down and hurt herself or lost her puppy. Similarly, she should be able to describe how a person is feeling in a specific context. For example, with his father's help, Scott labeled the feelings of the child who wanted candy in the store. It is also important that she identify her own feelings as they occur. She should be able to say that she is happy when she is going swimming, or sad when she loses a game.

People often feel more than one emotion at a time and your child should learn to recognize this. For example, she should be able to understand that a child might be happy to be starting first grade, but sad that summer is over. She also needs to realize that not everyone has the same reaction to a situation. For example, if a child is lost in a store, she will feel scared and her parent will feel worried.

Finally, you want to ensure that your child knows basic social responses, including greeting another person and answering social questions such as whether she has a pet and where she goes to school (see Chapter 3). She should also be able to tell the difference between actual objects and their play representations, as discussed in Chapter 2.

Teaching Basic Perspective Taking Skills

There are two major challenges in the early stage of learning perspective taking. The first is to understand that perception is relative—that is, that it depends upon who you are, what you see, what you experience, etc. The second major challenge is to understand that the context of an event is important. In other words, no single event can be interpreted or understood in a vacuum. Many variables affect the outcome of an event, including individual perceptions, environmental variables, and emotions.

To help children master these challenges, we start with three basic programs when teaching perspective taking: 1) field of vision, 2) perception versus non-perception, and 3) pretending. These tasks require the simplest forms of social understanding and create a foundation for more complex forms of perspective taking.

Field of Vision Task

One element of early perspective taking is understanding that others might not be able to see things exactly as you do. Your child needs to learn she may not be able to perceive something either because of circumstance or because of her orientation to the object. The basic program to teach this understanding is called a "field of vision perspective taking program."

In the field of vision task, your child will learn to identify her own and another person's perspectives relative to an object in a field of vision. For example, if you are facing a flower and your child has her back to it, you can see it, but she cannot. To teach this program, your child sits side by side next to her instructor, but facing opposite directions. In other words, your child and the instructor are sitting side by side, touching shoulders, but your child is faced 180 degrees in the opposite direction from the instructor. Objects are placed in front of both your child and her instructor. As shown in Table 4-2 on the next page, your child is asked several questions regarding field of vision such as "Can I (the instructor) see the cup?" If your child needs help recognizing what the instructor can and cannot see, let her try sitting in the instructor's position.

Table 4-2	Field of Vision Sample Questions
I see the _____. What do I see? What do you see?
Can I see the _____? (referring to an object visible only to instructor)
Can I see the _____? (referring to an object visible only to child)
Can you see the _____? (referring to an object visible only to child)
Can you see the _____? (referring to an object visible only to instructor)
Who can see the _____?

A strategy that helps some children to acquire this skill is to first introduce the program with dolls or puppets. This may be especially useful for children who have difficulty using pronouns. Two characters should be set up as you would two people (as described above). In this program, your child would be situated so that she can see both characters and both objects, and is then asked questions about what the characters can see. Next the program can be done with your child and a character, and then with your child and her instructor. When you use this sequential strategy, the pronouns "you" and "I" are introduced after the concept of visual perspective taking has been mastered. Having your child hold the item she is looking at (e.g., keep the cup in her hands) can also help her understand the concept of perspective taking. This strategy may build on previous programs, such as those describing items in possession (i.e., "I have____" versus "John has ___").

Pretending

Another early form of perspective taking involves understanding that two people may view the function of an object differently—specifically, that an object may be seen for what it really is, as well as for what someone is pretending that it is. For example, a paper bowl can be a hat in pretend play. This skill, which we describe in more detail in Chapter 2, is related to the development of abstract thought and of symbolic and representational play.

In the perspective taking program, your child learns to identify an object by its imaginary use. This requires that she have the ability to pretend and understand the pretend meaning of actions. If she needs help in developing some of the basic skills in this area you can use programs from Chapter 2.

In using pretend skills for perspective taking, your child is shown pictures or role plays of people engaging in pretend play activities. The people are using illogical items such as a banana to represent a telephone. It is helpful to use photographs of people and toys with which your child is familiar. For example, you can have a picture of a sibling using the toy banana your child sees every day. Your child is asked to label both the actual item and the action represented in pretend. For instance, you would show a photo of a person with a bowl on her head and say, "What is it?" "What is she pretending it is?" Table 4-3 on the next page has examples of the use of objects for pretend functions.

Balance the illogical scenes with examples of items being used logically to help your child learn the concept and not merely learn sequences of response patterns.

Perception vs. Non-perception

The perception vs. non-perception program helps your child understand when she can see something and when she cannot.

Table 4-3 | Objects to Use in Pretending

- Using a banana as a phone
- Using a bowl as a hat
- Using a toothbrush as a pencil
- Using a hairbrush as a microphone
- Using a plate as a steering wheel
- Using a straw as a toothbrush
- Using an empty paper towel holder as a horn
- Using a pen as an airplane
- Using a cup as an ice cream cone
- Using a block as a sandwich

This is a fairly subtle skill involving understanding one's experience, and it requires attention to the possibility of perception.

There are a variety of ways to manipulate the environment to enable or prevent your child from seeing an object. For example, an item might be in a closed box, behind a curtain, or inside an opaque jar. Alternately, the item can be in view, either in the open or in an open box or jar. This is a bit more complex than the field of vision task, when your child truly could not see the object. In this case, she needs to evaluate whether an object in front of her is visible, depending on its presentation.

Your child can be seated at a small desk or table. Place an object on the table or in the middle of the room, in full view. Alternately, you can put an object on the table before your child is seated. Ask your child whether she can see the object. Next, she can learn to respond when she is prevented from seeing the object, for example, when you have placed a bicycle behind a curtain. When an object is obscured from view, your child should indicate that she cannot see the object. Initially, you would hide the object before your child entered the room. In later stages of the program, you would let her observe you hiding the object, and then ask if she can see it.

Teaching Intermediate Perspective Taking Skills

After your child masters the fundamentals of perspective taking, teaching will follow several different paths. One focus is on expanding her understanding of the difference between appearance and reality. You will also teach the social information that we convey with eye contact. In this intermediate stage of perspective taking, some nuances of understanding social information are introduced. These form the basis for later, more complex forms of social understanding. Your child also begins to acquire information to help her decode social situations, interpret cues, and react appropriately to other people.

As Table 4-4 indicates, there are four programs in this intermediate stage of learning about perspective taking.

Table 4-4 | Intermediate Perspective Taking Programs

◆ Appearance versus Reality	◆ Non-Logical Placement
◆ Lining up	◆ Utility of Eye Gaze

Appearance versus Reality

In the appearance versus reality program, your child learns to discriminate the apparent versus real qualities of an object. In the simplest task of this program, an object is wrapped in colored cellophane paper that makes it appear to be of that color. The object is then unwrapped, and shown to be a different color. As Table 4-5 on the next page indicates, to do this program you sit facing your child and show her an object such as a block wrapped in transparent, colored paper. You ask her, "What color is the block?" Then you unwrap the object and say, "What color is the block really?" Next, you re-wrap the block and say, "What color is the block really?"

Table 4-5 | Questions for Appearance Versus Reality Program—Instructor Guiding Process

Child is presented with an object wrapped in colored paper:
Adult: What color is the _____?

Child is presented with an unwrapped object:
Adult: What color is the _____ really?

Child is presented with a re-wrapped object.
Adult: What color is it really?

Table 4-6 | Questions for Appearance Versus Reality—Child Unwraps

Child is presented with an object wrapped in colored paper:
Adult: What color does it look like?
Adult: What color is it really?

After your child masters the sequence in which you unwrap the objects for her, the next step is for her to do the unwrapping. As shown in Table 4-6, you hand her an object, ask her the color, and then ask her what color it is really. Her task is to unwrap the paper to determine the object's true color. Table 4-7 lists objects to use for this activity. Be sure to use different colors of covering paper as well as objects. You can expand this program to include objects in the shape of other known objects. In this case, your child is asked, "What does this look like?" and "What is it really?" For example, you might give her a wax candle in the shape of an apple (see Table 4-8).

Illogical Placement

This program introduces your child to the logical assumptions that people make about the content of containers. As a consequence, she learns that her personal knowledge of what is re-

Table 4-7 | Items to Be Used in Appearance Versus Reality—Color

- Pen in red cellophane paper (or plastic wrap)
- Pen in blue cellophane paper
- Pen in green cellophane paper
- Pen in yellow cellophane paper
- Block in red tissue paper
- Block in blue tissue paper
- Block in green tissue paper
- Block in yellow tissue paper

Table 4-8 | Sample Items to Be Used in Appearance Versus Reality—Function (What is it really?)

- Candle in the shape of an apple
- Candle in the shape of a baseball
- Candle in the shape of a flower
- Pen in the shape of a fish
- Pen in the shape of a baseball bat

Note: There are many possibilities within this program, as many objects come "disguised" as other things. Explore candles, soaps, erasers, and chocolates.

ally in the containers is not universal. For example, if you asked for something to eat and were given a closed, brand name box of donuts you would expect donuts. However, I might have put teabags in the box as a prank and I would know you were not going to find donuts.

The illogical placement program is an extension of the appearance versus reality program. It requires your child to indicate what another person will guess in a given context, in light of her experience.

To teach this program, the instructor places an object inside a box or container that is not usually found in that container. For example, he might put pretzels in a crayon box. As shown in Table 4-9, your child is then asked "What do you think is in the box?" She is directed to open the box and asked, "What is really in the box?" Finally she is asked, "What will Dad think is in the box?" Table 4-10 suggests common objects to use for this task. Your child must be able to recognize the typical function of these containers and be able to label the objects to do this program.

If your child has difficulty understanding that others will expect the logical item, several different strategies may help her. First, you can provide additional preliminary questions such as "What is usually in a crayon box?" It may also help your child to watch peers predict (correctly) what someone else will think is in the box.

One caution: it is possible that your child may over-apply the illogical placement program. For example, some children will begin to expect that the unexpected always occurs, and may fail to anticipate usual consequences. It is important to present this as a guessing game, so that it is clearly a novel scenario. Furthermore, you should mix in instances in which the expected items indeed appear in their usual locations (i.e., there is no surprise this time).

Table 4-9 | It Is Not What You Expect!—Illogical
Placement of Objects

Adult: "What do you think is in the box?"
Child predicts what is in the box. Child opens box or container.
Adult: "What is really in the box?"
Adult: "What will (Dad/Mom) think is in the box?"

Table 4-10 | Objects for Use in Illogical Placement
Programs

◆ Crayon box	◆ Cereal box
◆ Chips bag	◆ Coin purse
◆ Tape case	◆ Juice box
◆ Lunchbox	◆ Tissue box
◆ Egg container	◆ Pudding container

Lining Up

Another intermediate program addresses orienting one's body correctly to "line up." This program revisits the issue of orientation to materials that was first addressed in the "Field of Vision" and "Perception versus Non-perception" programs. Now, however, you will work on the school-related skill of lining up appropriately with peers. Most children with autism have limited experience with this classroom skill. Furthermore, it involves a unique set of expectations that differs from other everyday situations such as circle time or play time.

This program is done in several ways, starting with dolls. To create a scenario about lining up, the instructor might ring a bell, and say, "Time to line up." The instructor then places the dolls sequentially in a line. One of the dolls is deliberately placed in an incorrect orientation, either facing 90 degrees (facing to the side) or 180 degrees (facing the opposite direction) from the other dolls' orientations. The instructor asks the child, "Is everyone lined up?" If she says "yes," she is asked, "Is everyone lined up correctly?" If she indicates there is an error, she is asked, "Who is lined up incorrectly?" and then "Can you fix it?" She is given a chance to fix the doll out of position and then again asked, "Is everyone lined up correctly?" As she gains experience, your child may give a correct full answer without the sequence of questions.

Before embarking on this program, your child needs to have the prerequisite skill of being able to identify correct orientation. Furthermore, you may want to provide a visual cue about correct orientation (e.g., line up the dolls facing the door.)

Although you can use dolls to start, it is important to generalize this skill to actually lining up. You may want to begin by having other children line up, without your child's participation. In this case, she continues to "observe" the lining up and evaluates the correctness of each participant's orientation. You would arrange ahead of time for one child's position to be incorrect. Your child's task is to help this child stand correctly. (You should brief this child ahead of time as to how to respond to your child's attempts at correction. For example, you may want her to do whatever your child asks, even if it is wrong, and to await correction by the teacher. In any case, the peer should know what to expect, who to listen to, and how to proceed.) The next step is to have your child participate in the lining up activity to be certain that she can do it.

Utility of Gaze

In this program, your child learns to identify which object a person wants by tracking that person's eye gaze. This skill extends the social understanding aspect of perspective taking.

To begin, the instructor shows your child a person (often in a line drawing or exaggerated picture) with a variety of objects around her. The person's eyes are clearly oriented toward one specific object. The goal is for your child to identify which object the person wants by following her gaze. This way, she learns that we can infer information about what people want by watching their eyes. To help her think about the meaning of eye gaze, you could ask, "What does Julia want?" or "What does Julia want to eat?" or "What is Julia wishing for?"

Many children with autism have particular difficulty understanding the information available through eye contact. This may be more true for children who avert their own gaze or who otherwise avoid looking into the eyes of others. In the box below, we describe the case of Brendan, a little boy who had a hard time grasping the meaning of gaze. Notice how fine grained our assessment of Brendan's learning pattern had to be in order to help him learn this skill. This type of painstaking attention to detail is often what is required for teaching subtle social skills. While you may feel like your child cannot learn a particular skill, it may be

---

The Eyes Have It

Brendan had a hard time understanding the utility of gaze program. He couldn't seem to understand that looking at an object could indicate a desire for that object. While it was hard for us to know what he was thinking, it seemed as if he might not be "tuning in" to where people were looking.

At first, his instructional team tried to increase the salience of the materials they used. They drew large-eyed children, whose eyes were directed very significantly toward a particular item. They also used arrows to show where the children were looking. While the arrows worked, they could never be faded. As soon as the arrows were removed, Brendan couldn't do the task. Clearly, he had learned to follow the arrows, not the eyes.

Next, the team decided to role play the task themselves. In the process, they developed a system of additional cues that was eventually successful.

At first, Brendan could only indicate what someone wanted if it was in that person's hand. Next, he learned to identify preference if the person was only reaching toward the item with an exaggerated outstretched arm. Then, he learned to look for this same pointing gesture, without the obvious reaching motion. The pointing gesture was then paired with an eye gaze. To do this in the role play, the instructor would place a finger by his or her eye, and gaze in the direction the finger pointed. Finally, the pointing was eliminated, and Brendan discovered the information simply from looking at the individual's eyes.

that a more microscopic analysis of the steps of learning will yield successful results.

Advanced Perspective Taking Skills

After your child masters the basic and intermediate skills, it is time for advanced perspective taking. As shown in Table 4-11, these programs teach more about the different experiences and knowledge people have, and how to recognize what is not logical about stories.

Table 4-11 | Advanced Perspective Taking Skills
◆ Differential experience—the concept that others' experiences may be similar to or different from one's own
◆ Differential knowledge—the concept that individuals vary in what they know about one another and about events
◆ Perspective Taking Game
◆ What's Wrong?

The concepts of differential knowledge or experience are expanded in this section. In the basic and intermediate programs, the focus was on what people can see depending on their physical orientation, and on their expectations when they have limited information (such as expecting to see crayons in a crayon box). For the advanced stage of programming, this perspective taking is extended into a game called the Perspective Taking Game. Another useful skill that will build on the basic visual scanning skills of the "lining up" program will help your child recognize and solve a variety of social mistakes.

Differential Experience

In the differential experience program, your child learns to recognize when her experience differs from another person's. This is a fundamental task of perspective taking because it requires that she understand that experience is not universal. For example, while I like carrot cake, you may not. While I like roller coasters, you may have never been on one. While Prague is my favorite city, you may never have been there. In other words, while I feel strongly about things and places I have experienced, others may have different opinions of

them or may have never experienced them. One of the greatest challenges in perspective taking for children with autism is understanding that the experiences of others may be different and distinct from their own.

We begin teaching this difference in perspective with photos of events such as family vacations, trips to the beach, and so forth. To begin the program, your child and an instructor who was not on the trip should look at a photo of a family outing. The instructor asks the child whether various people, including the child herself, the instructor, and other family members, had a good time at the event. Answering this question is a two-step process for your child. She must first recognize whether or not that person was at the event. She may then be asked to explain why that individual did or did not enjoy the event. For example, if the photo was of a family vacation and the question was whether the instructor enjoyed it, the instructor would say, "I wasn't there." (The reasons for not enjoying the event would be limited to not being present.) Table 4-12 on the next page has a list of questions to ask and Table 4-13 which follows, offers some suggestions for activities.

Table 4-12 | Sample Instructions for Differential
Experience Program with Photos

Adult: "Did you have a good time at the (zoo, beach, etc.)?" "Why?"
Adult: "Did I have a good time at the (zoo, beach, etc.)?" "Why?"
Adult: "Did Mommy (Daddy, Grandma) have a good time at the
(zoo, beach, etc.)?" "Why?"

Table 4-13 | Sample Events for Differential
Experience Program

- Beach
- Zoo
- School Picnic
- Disney World
- Birthday Party
- Dentist's Office (presence, not enjoyment)
- Getting a Shot (presence, not enjoyment)

The more important component of this skill is recognizing whether certain individuals shared an experience. This is more important than being able to say whether someone had a good time. If your child cannot recall whether someone enjoyed herself, but can recall that she was there, you may decide to consider the skill mastered. Alternately, you can ask your child to go find out from that person whether she enjoyed herself. In this way, you can also be building skills in getting information (discussed in Chapter 3).

In the beginning, the photos should be of events in which your child was a participant. However, once she masters that task, you need to add pictures of events in which she was not a participant. The family photos from an instructor or friend who is not part of social activities with your child are a good source of such pictures. With this material, your child learns to answer questions about events she did not experience. This can eventually be extended to asking questions about weekend activities, sports participation, TV shows watched, etc.

Differential Knowledge

In the differential knowledge program, your child learns to evaluate questions based on whether she possesses the knowledge to answer them. For example, you might ask her, "Did I have a bagel for breakfast?" Your child should appropriately answer, "I don't know" if, in fact, she does not know what you had for breakfast because she was not there.

There are two main scenarios in this program. Your child either a) does not know the person you are inquiring about, or b) does not know the information you are requesting. Table 4-14 lists questions to ask your child to pose challenges about differential knowledge.

It is important to mix questions about unknown material with known information so that your child will not learn to say, "I don't

---

Table 4-14 | Sample Questions for Differential Knowledge Program

- Do you know my friend _____? (looking at a photo of an unknown person)
- Do you like my friend _____? (looking at a photo of an unknown person)
- Does he have any sisters? (looking at a photo of an unknown person)
- Does he have a cat? (looking at a photo of an unknown person)
- Does she like roller coasters? (looking at a photo of an unknown person)
- What did I have for breakfast?
- What did I do this weekend?
- Do I like chocolate ice cream?
- Do I like Rug Rats?
- Do I like the color green?
- Do I have any brothers?
- Do I have a dog?

know" to every item. The critical task is for her to evaluate whether she knows the person or the information. It should, therefore, be taught as a distinction between situations in which she knows the information and situations in which she does not. If your child is incorrect, you would correct her with the answer and with the appropriate explanation. For example, if you ask her, "Do I have a dog?" and she guesses no, you might say, "You don't know whether or not I have a dog. You've never been to my house."

This program can also be used as an opportunity to reinforce the skill of obtaining information (for example, by asking Mommy, "Do you like green?"). However, this would not typically be done in the early stages of acquisition.

Perspective Taking Game

The Perspective Taking Game builds on the concepts of differential experience and knowledge. In this program, the "theory of mind" deficits that we described at the beginning of this chapter are addressed. To play this game, your child identifies where another person thinks an object is, based on the information available to that person and to herself. You may recognize this as a reenactment of the "Sally-Ann" task in the discussion of theory of mind. The game requires that your child distinguish between her own knowledge and the knowledge of another person to highlight the difference between herself and the other person.

This game is played with two children, one of whom is a peer. A sibling is a great choice for this program, as it is usually fun. Another child with autism may not be a good choice, as he or she is also unlikely to possess the skill. First, with both children present, the instructor takes an object such as a cup and hides it in a specific place. To make sure they are paying attention to where she hides it, the instructor asks each child where the cup is after it has been hidden. One child is then asked to leave the room. The instructor (or the child who remains) then moves the object. The child who remains is then asked, "Where does _____ think the cup is?" The correct response is the original location of the object. If the child gives this answer, it indicates that she understands that the other youngster does not know the new location.

There are several variations of this game. For example, before the second child returns to the room, the instructor can ask the child with autism, "Where is the cup now?" "Where was the cup before we moved it?" and "Where will _____ think it is?" The instructor can ask the returning child where she thinks the cup is before she asks the remaining child. This allows for observational learning of the concept, as the returning child indicates her expectation before the remaining child is asked to state it.

This task can be made more complex. For example, several objects can be placed, but only one object moved. Items can also disappear—for example, a cookie can be eaten. In another version, Child A puts pudding in her lunchbox and goes to get her book bag. Child B takes out the pudding, and puts in cake. What does Child A expect to find in her lunchbox?

The task can be altered to include giving crucial information to only one child about how to find a hidden object. For example, two children may be told that an item is going to be hidden. One child then leaves the room, while the remaining child is told that the object will be hidden in the bookcase. The remaining child stays in the room and observes the relocation of the object. When the other child returns, both children guess where the item is hidden. The child who remained can be asked where the other child will think the object might be. When the child understands that only she will guess it is in the bookcase, she will have learned that the information was differentially provided.

In another variation of this game using three children, Child A is in a particular hiding spot when Child B leaves the room. Then Child A gets out of the hiding spot, and Child C enters the hiding spot. The question is, whom does Child B expect to find in the hiding spot?

The potential for frustration exists in this game. It is important to reward all participants for effort and sportsmanship. For example, if an edible treat was hidden, let all participants have a piece of it when it is retrieved from the final location.

Occasionally, a child may consistently make errors in this game. If this happens with your child, make sure that your teaching efforts are making learning as errorless as possible. You can provide the correct information in a variety of ways, prior to even posing a question to your child, through prompting, peer modeling, etc. For instance, remember that you can ask the returning child where she thinks the hidden item is before you ask the other child to predict what the returning child will say. If, however, your child is experiencing tremendous difficulty in mastering this concept, it may be best to discontinue the program and try again in a few months.

What's Wrong?

The impact of social skill deficits on children with autism in typical classrooms is vivid to us from our work helping children make this transition to school. One of us (MJW) was consulted about Andrew, who was doing fine with the academic work in class, but was struggling socially, according to the teacher. He did not always look at people when he answered them, and sometimes he interrupted children when they were talking and playing. She was concerned that he didn't "get" some of the social rules.

Andrew's experience is not unusual. While many children succeed academically in school placements, the social realm is typically more challenging. There are many "unwritten rules" that children are expected to follow in social situations. These behaviors are hard to identify and challenging to teach. Social interaction inevitably involves perspective taking. We must be able to perceive other people's situations, to anticipate their preferences, and to predict their reactions.

One way to assist children like Andrew in comprehending another person's perspective is to identify appropriate and inappropriate means of interacting in very concrete terms. Andrew did much better in picking up the social rules when we gave him visual examples of these rules, and helped him learn to identify when they were and were not being followed. For Andrew, the most important social expectations involved eye contact. We presented him with examples of people looking at one another while talking, looking up when someone entered the room, making eye contact when greeted, looking at others when saying goodbye, etc.

Just as you told your child to "fix" what was wrong when she lined up dolls incorrectly, you can help her identify and correct errors in social interaction. When a child with autism understands the expectations for such interactions, it becomes easier to connect successfully with others. This particular strategy was reviewed in the description of role plays in Chapter 3. We will quickly review the concept again here.

"What's Wrong?" is a program to teach your child to recognize common social errors. You may begin by playing out scenarios with dolls or puppets. Later, however, it is important to generalize to live role plays in which your child is a participant. You can ask your child to observe a role play scenario, and then to identify whether there were any problems in it. If there were problems, you can ask her to identify the problem and to fix it. You can then re-play the scenario with the change, and ask her whether it is now correct. Some children enjoy orchestrating the corrected role play themselves, either with the dolls or through live modeling. These methods of rehearsing the correct way to interact can be excellent ways to reinforce a social concept. As shown in Table 4-15 on the next page, these scenarios should focus on social problems faced by your child. For example, if your child has trouble with eye contact or speaking in an appropriate tone of voice, these would be acted out.

Of course, just because your child knows how to act in theory doesn't always mean that she will do so in practice. Your child may be able to identify the error in a role play, fix it in a follow-up exercise, and still have trouble consistently demonstrating the skill in daily life. She may lose sight of the error when engaged in the complexity of a real social interaction. Bear in mind that there are many other ways in which we might be simultaneously addressing a given skill deficit. This is just one approach. It is helpful for many children to learn to concretely identify such difficulties. This teaching activity helps to highlight the specific skills that may be absent or inconsistently demonstrated.

Table 4-15 | Some Common Targets for the "What's Wrong" Program

- Making eye contact with your conversational partner
- Facing your conversational partner
- Keeping hands appropriately quiet while talking
- Speaking in an audible voice
- Speaking at a comprehensible pace
- Asking politely to interrupt ("Excuse me")
- Failing to respond
- Responding out of context (e.g., answering different questions than those asked, providing irrelevant answers to questions)
- Responding to common occurrences (e.g., sneezes)
- Responding to distress

Teaching Extensions of Advanced Perspective Taking Skills

Because children with autism need to develop more sophisticated perspective taking skills as they get older, they may need continued teaching in this area. One essential skill to learn is identifying truth and lies. It is critically important for your child to recognize false information for both social and safety reasons. Another critical challenge is the development of empathy and compassion. Children who lack these skills will have a limited capacity for deep friendship, and may be perceived by others as insensitive. As shown in Table 4-16, in this section we describe three extensions of advanced perspective taking skills to teach the fundamentals of recognizing falsehoods and learning compassion.

False Information

Learning to recognize false information prepares your child to recognize lies and may also enhance her sense of humor as she recognizes the absurd in statements. Table 4-17 shows some of the areas to target in teaching the concept of false information.

We introduced the fundamentals of this concept in Chapter 3 when we described encouraging assertive behavior. However, in the present chapter the focus is on recognizing false information in order to identify lies and cheating.

The simplest way to introduce the concept of false information is to begin with personal and logical information, such as name, age, gender, and items in possession. In this program, your child asks her instructor a series of questions to which she knows the answer. These would include things like "What is your name?" "How old are you?" "Are you a boy or a girl?" "What color is your shirt?" A second instructor (or parent) assists the child with posing the questions. He or she also helps your child evaluate the veracity of the answers by asking her one or more of the following questions: 1) Is that the truth? 2) Is that true? 3) Is that true or false? 4) Is that false? or Is that a lie? The instructor may lay the groundwork for later programs by commenting on the lying and indicating that it is not nice.

This program can be extended to information about the location of hidden objects. In this sequence, your child enters the

Table 4-16	Extensions of Advanced Perspective Taking Programs

- Identification of False Information
- Identification of Lying and Cheating
- Development of Empathy and Compassion

Table 4-17	Identification of False Information

Logical Information	**Location of Items**
• Name	*Inferential*
• Age	• Impossible tasks
• Gender	• Unlikely events
• Items in possession	

room and the first adult asks, "Do you want the (toy or candy)?" If your child indicates that she wants the item, the instructor states its hidden location, for example, "It's in the toy box." When your child goes to the toy box, she will find it empty. At this point, the second adult says to your child, "It's not there. Did he tell us the truth about where it is?" The goal is for your child to indicate that the information was false. The second adult then asks the first adult where the object really is, or encourages your child to do so, and helps her get it, if need be.

Another way to provide false information regarding the location of items is in the context of the perspective taking game we described above. Since this is a familiar task, it may be a good way to introduce the concept. In this case, the instructor provides false information about the new location of the target object to the returning child. A second instructor can assist your child in identifying the information as false.

The identification of false information can be extended to the inferential realm. In other words, your child can learn to guess that information is not true. In the beginning, you will target concrete and very unlikely events. The instructor presents absurd or unlikely information in a social conversation, and your child is helped to identify the information as false. In this sequence, the first adult says to your child, "Guess what?" When your child says "What?" the adult responds with something absurd such as, "I just got back from Mars." If necessary, the second adult prompts your child to question the absurd information. She might ask, "Does that sound possible?" or she might simply model disbelief. The goal is for your child to respond appropriately with, "No way," "Yeah, right," or laughter. Examples of impossible and unlikely events are listed in Table 4-18.

In using these activities to teach your child about false information, it is important to guard against the development of mistrust. It is imperative that you make it clear to your child when you are beginning one of these activities, perhaps by giving them names such as "The Maybe Game" or the "Backwards" game and then telling your child that it is time to play that game. It is also important to sprinkle the activity with situations in which the teacher is telling the truth. The instructor can say, "Oh, that one was real." Generally, however, if your child possesses prerequisite skills and has a foundation of perspective taking skills, she is able to make the "cognitive leap." She will understand that her teacher may play this game with her, but remains a trustworthy and honest friend.

Table 4-18 | Impossible or Unlikely Events to Teach False Information

Impossible Events
(Note: It is helpful, especially in the beginning stages of this program, to alter your voice or give some other cue that the information about to be presented may be silly.)

- Child driving a car
- Going to Mars on vacation
- Lifting a refrigerator
- Touching the sky
- Walking on water
- Flying in the backyard

Unlikely Events
- Child eating 10 cheeseburgers
- Going swimming in the ocean when it's snowing
- Winning a race running against a car

Telling Lies

After your child can recognize false information, she needs to learn about socially undesirable behaviors that depend on falsehood such as dishonesty, lying, and cheating. Although people with autism rarely engage in these kinds of deceptions, she needs to understand these behaviors because she may encounter them among her peers. It is also important for her to avoid doing these things herself. (Parents, however, are usually thrilled when their child with autism lies. It is a major step in the direction of typical behavior!)

A critically important element in these lessons is learning why people do these things. It is important for your child to be able to talk about why an individual might cheat or lie, because understanding what motivates people to behave in unfair ways is an aspect of empathy. It also becomes increasingly important in academic realms as children move into middle and high school and begin to study literature that involves complex motives. Table 4-19 summarizes the skills to be taught in learning about deception.

Table 4-19 | Recognizing Dishonesty, Lying, and Cheating

Identification of Lying
  ◆ To prevent negative consequences
  ◆ For self gain

Identification of cheating
  ◆ In games
  ◆ On academic tasks

You already introduced the concept of dishonesty to your child in the identification of false information programs. Now you can help her identify situations in which people lie. She needs to recognize that the two main reasons people lie are to prevent negative consequences or for personal gain. (A more complicated motivation, to avoid hurting someone else's feelings, is much more subtle. Usually children who have been able to learn these simpler concepts will be able to understand the "little white lie" too, at a later stage of development.) The easiest way to introduce these concepts is with simple vignettes such as those shown in Table 4-20.

When you read a vignette to your child, emphasize several points. The first point is that the child in the episode is lying. The second point is that she is lying for a reason—namely, to avoid

Table 4-20 | Vignettes for Teaching about Lies

A Dog's Tale

Sammy was chasing the dog around the dining room table. They were running really fast. On one turn, Sammy lost his balance. He knocked into the table, and the vase toppled over, fell on the floor, and broke into lots of tiny little pieces. When Sammy's mom saw the mess, she called all the children together, and demanded an explanation. She said, "Who did this?" No one answered. She asked each of them individually. When she came to Sammy, she said, "Sammy, are you responsible for this?" Sammy shook his head no, and said, "No, Mom. It wasn't me."

Dressed Up but Not Grown Up

Alexis and Kim were having a great time playing after school. They started playing dress up with all of Kim's mother's things. They found her cosmetics too, and got lipstick all over their faces and the clothes. Alexis really liked Kim's Mom's perfumes, and took one home. When Kim's Mom came home, she saw that there was lipstick on her favorite dress. She asked Kim if she knew how it got there. Kim said, "I don't know. How should I know?" A week later Kim and Alexis were playing again. Kim's Mom was getting ready to go out, and couldn't find her perfume. She went to both girls and asked them if they had seen it. Both girls said no.

The Dog Ate it!

Evan forgot all about his writing assignment. He never thought of it last night after the baseball game. When Mrs. Jones told all the students to pass their assignment forward, he was really worried. He went up to Mrs. Jones and told her that his dog Frisky ate his assignment this morning, and that he didn't have time to do it all over again before the bus came.

What's for Lunch?

Today is peanut butter and jelly day in the cafeteria. Jake doesn't like peanut butter and jelly sandwiches. He likes pizza. He knows that you can get pizza if you can't have peanut butter. He tells the cafeteria worker that he is allergic to peanut butter, and can't have the sandwich. She makes him pizza instead.

More for Me

All of the children have been eating cupcakes at Emily's birthday party. Hannah wants another cupcake. Emily's Mom said only one per person. Hannah tells Emily's Mom that she didn't get one, so that she can have a second one.

I'm Forever Blowing Bubbles

Kyle and Christopher were playing with the bubble maker all day. Kyle knows that Chris will want to take it to camp tomorrow. Kyle wants to be able to play with it again at home. Kyle hides the bubble maker behind the shed. Christopher looks everywhere for the bubble maker before camp the next morning. He asks Kyle to help him find it. Kyle pretends to look, and never tells Chris where it is.

negative consequences or to get what she wants. It is helpful if you elaborate on the negative consequences the child may fear. You should also discuss what she should have done such as telling the truth, or apologizing for her wrongdoing.

You can help your child choose the right course of action by listing all of the alternatives, anticipating the consequences of each course of action, and choosing the best option (as was touched on in Chapter 3 in the section on problem solving). Anticipating the negative consequences of each choice is a very important element in this problem solving. Your child needs to understand that telling lies fosters mistrust, and makes it more likely that she will be suspected of wrongdoing in the future. Honesty, on the other hand, fosters trust and forgiveness. Table 4-21 lists sample questions to help your child explore the meaning of each vignette.

It is sometimes, though not usually, helpful to begin with stories that bear little resemblance to your child's experience. This

---

Table 4-21 | Sample Questions to Help Your Child Think about Lies

To define the problem
- Is he/she telling the truth?
- Is he/she lying?
- Why is he/she lying?
- What is he/she afraid might happen if he/she tells the truth? (fear of negative consequence scenarios)
- What is he/she hoping to get/getting by lying? (personal gain scenarios)
- What might happen as a result of lying?
- What might happen if he/she told the truth?

For problem solving
- What are all the choices? Let's list them.
- What would happen with each choice? (List all possible consequences.)
- What is the best choice?

may be the case if your child is very fearful about her own wrong-doings or gets extremely anxious about discussing them.

When your child lies in real life, it is important to react appropriately. These are golden opportunities to teach a lesson in morality. Always emphasize the importance of honesty and fairness when these issues arise.

Cheating

As with lying, your child needs to be able to identify cheating and also understand the motivation for cheating. For example, your child should learn that people may cheat to win, to do well, and so forth. Our programs focus on cheating in two settings: during game play and at school.

The identification of cheating in games is fairly straightforward, and can be enacted in play activities. To teach these skills, the instructors need to deliberately cheat at times. This is necessary to give sufficient practice in understanding the concepts. Cheating can also be enacted in role play scenarios or vignettes. Table 4-22 below lists some of the ways you can cheat, such as taking extra spaces in moving around a game board or peeking at cards on the stack. As was the case for telling lies, there are questions you can ask to help your child think about what is wrong with cheating. In all cases, you should emphasize the definition of cheating as a violation of the rules of the game. Sample questions are shown in Table 4-23 on the next page.

Cheating also needs to be explained in the context of school. Children often cheat on class work, homework assignments, and

---

Table 4-22 | Ways to Cheat on Games

- Violations of turn taking protocol (e.g., taking an extra turn)
- Going extra spaces to get to a desired location in a board game
- Taking too many cards (or not enough cards) in a card game
- Peeking at the cards other players have in a card game
- Peeking at cards ahead of time (from communal pile)

Table 4-23 | Questions to Guide Thinking
about Cheating

Defining the Problem:
- Is that OK?
- What's wrong?
- Is that fair?
- Why is that unfair?
- Is that cheating?
- What rule is being broken?
- Why is that a good rule?

Problem Solving:
- What are all the choices? Let's list them.
- What would happen with each choice? (List all possible consequences.)
- What is the best choice?

---

tests, and children with autism are often unwitting victims of cheating when other children copy their work. They may also cheat themselves without realizing the seriousness of the offense. In fact, if a child has become good at learning by watching others, she may see children cheat and copy that behavior just as she copies their desirable behaviors!

It is essential to emphasize the rules regarding cheating. These can be reviewed at logical times, such as before group games or before a test. It is also important to distinguish between times when working with peers to get an answer is acceptable, such as during a group assignment, and times when working with peers is forbidden, such as on an individual spelling test. Strategies to prevent cheating, such as keeping one's eyes on one's own paper and covering one's answers, should also be discussed. The use of such strategies is proactive, and significantly reduces the occurrence of cheating.

It is also important to emphasize the concept of pride in one's own work. This can be done incidentally in a variety of ways. It can be modeled by parents and siblings. It can also be suggested by a parent when a child's work is being admired (e.g., "Wow. You must be proud.") Similarly, if you discuss tests as opportunities for feedback on her performance, your child can view feedback as additional learning opportunities.

Just as with lies, it is important to help your child understand why people cheat. As suggested in Table 4-23, it is also helpful to use a problem-solving framework to address situations where one might cheat so your child can learn different solutions.

Apologies

The final programs in this section address teaching empathy and compassion. The more adept your child becomes in these areas, the smoother her relationships with other children and adults will become. However, as is true for the other skills in this chapter, you need to "think small" and set modest goals. While your child may be a long way from feeling true empathy for others, she can begin the journey by taking small steps in increasing her consideration for others.

We start with apologies for physically hurting another child or breaking something that belongs to her because this is a relatively explicit behavior. When a child says that she is sorry for hurting someone, she is acknowledging that her actions caused distress to someone else. This concrete expression of regret over physical actions can be introduced in role plays or in vignettes. To help your child think about the situation, you can ask questions such as, "What should she say?" "Why should she say that?" "How does her friend feel?" "What can she say to make her friend feel better?"

Eventually, your child needs to progress to expressing regret for hurting others in non-physical ways. Your child needs to learn that we hurt people with our words and with our failure to act. Some of the scenarios you might act out here include name-calling, failing to invite someone to a party, and not answering when someone asks you to play. The issue of "white lies" briefly mentioned in the previous section may also be addressed in this context. That is, you may be able to help your child understand that white lies may be motivated by the desire to avoid hurting others.

To help your child think about regret both for causing physical harm and emotional harm, read the vignettes in Table 4-24. Discuss with your child how the child in the scenario could have acted differently. Also take advantage of any naturally occurring events in your child's life that call for an apology. For example, tell your child "I'm sorry" if you inadvertently step on her heel or knock down her block tower. Also, prompt your child to apologize if events warrant it. For example, ask her to, "Please tell your brother you're sorry," if she accidentally breaks something of his. Also be sure to keep lines of communication open with the school, and get specific information regarding your child's social relationships on a daily basis. You can create stories or role plays about events at school to generate discussions about what happened, how the individuals felt, and what could have been done differently.

Showing Compassion

In Chapter 3, we introduced the notion of social convention when responding to another person's needs. These programs are extended here to help your child build a greater capacity for

compassion. By helping your child learn to express concern for people in need or distress, you will also be helping her form one of the building blocks for friendship. (Note: If your child has not yet gained control over her own emotions, or is very upset by the emotional displays of others, she is probably not ready for this skill.)

Table 4-24 | Vignettes for Teaching Children about Apologizing

Gene and Eric were playing in the hammock, taking turns. Gene was pushing Eric on the swing. He pushed him hard, and the hammock started swinging faster and higher. Eric got scared, and tried to crawl off. He got to the edge, and the whole hammock turned over and flipped him onto the ground. It hurt when he bumped his head, and he was really scared. Gene didn't mean to do it, but he still felt badly that Eric was scared and hurt.

Leyone took James's electronic space phone to school for show and tell. All of the children loved it, especially the button that said, "Prepare for transport." It was the most popular show-and-tell item of the day. Then Leyone took it on the playground, so all of the kids could see it again. She put it in her pocket when they were done playing with it, and started playing tag. Once, when she was running really fast, the phone fell out of her pocket. It hit the hard cement of the playground and broke. She pressed the buttons to see if they worked, but the toy made no noise. She was so sad. She knew her brother would be very upset when he heard the news.

Peter was very upset that he couldn't play Nintendo. His babysitter wanted to watch her favorite show, and she said he could play it in an hour. He got really angry, and he stomped around the house. His babysitter didn't say anything. Then he said to his babysitter, "I hate you." He could see how his words hurt his sitter's feelings. She looked like she might cry.

Laura and Lisa were both playing with the kitchen set. Lenny came over and asked, "Can I play cooking with you guys?" Laura and Lisa just kept playing, getting out the pots and pans. Lenny asked again, but they didn't answer. Lenny looked sad. He watched them play for a few minutes, and then he went over to the block area.

One element of compassion is responding to others when they are showing clear signs of physical or emotional distress. Table 4-25 lists some events that can be built into role plays or scenarios where compassion can be learned. While responses to some of the situations are fairly self-evident, it is not always clear how to demonstrate compassion in a particular situation. For more ambiguous or complex circumstances, you can teach your child multiple, appropriate responses. For example, if someone gets a cut, your child can either ask if they are OK, offer to get help, or offer to get a band-aid. Some children might even learn to do some assessment of the person's needs in a problem solving format.

It is one thing to respond in the moment to someone who is clearly indicating that she is hurt or upset. It is quite another to remain concerned about that person after the initial display of distress has faded. Yet, recalling that someone has been in distress is an important element of compassion. We "check in" with one an-

---

Table 4-25 | Opportunities to Show Compassion

- Saying "ouch"
- Scraping a knee
- Falling off a swing
- Falling off a slide
- Bumping head on desk
- Obviously stubbing a toe
- Getting a paper cut
- Twisting an ankle
- Getting stung by a bee
- Complaining about a headache
- Clutching stomach with a stomachache
- Crying
- Saying "I just can't do it"
- Saying "I can't find it anywhere"
- Saying "This is too hard"
- Saying "I give up"

other, and follow up when someone has clearly been distressed. This is a skill that needs to be taught to children with autism.

Learning this extended expression of concern can be facilitated through role play. An instructor may, in the early moments of an instructional session, complain of having a particular physical ailment such as a headache. At several points throughout the session, your child can be prompted to inquire about the headache. In fact, she can be reminded to inquire about the headache the next day as well. It is probably best if these reminders are nonverbal cues, such as pictures or a sentence strip. The sentence strip might say "How are you feeling now?" or "Is your headache better?" A verbal prompt will likely be more difficult to fade and teaches your child to rely on others for such reminders. A simple question mark on your child's desk may be enough of a cue to inquire about anything important from the previous day. Naturally, the goal is to fade all such reminders over time.

One possible side effect of teaching your child to express concern may be that she will make too many inquiries and annoy the person she is trying to comfort. If so, it may be necessary to teach her when to stop expressing concern. For example, if you asked about the headache and it is better, no further follow-ups are needed. Such rules can be introduced as needed.

It should be noted that concern and empathy can be communicated nonverbally as well. Children who cannot express sympathy vocally may be able to use an augmentative communication device to do so. They could also show concern through actions, such as by offering a hug or patting someone on the shoulder.

End Note

Many of the skills in this chapter are difficult for children with autism. While some children will find them intrinsically rewarding, others will struggle through the teaching activities. It is important to evaluate how your child reacts to these teaching activities, and to make sure you are rewarding her sufficiently for her efforts.

You may feel a little awkward as you embark on teaching these skills. You may suddenly become self-conscious about your own behavior (e.g., telling a white lie). While it is helpful to model appropriate behavior for your child, it is also important to use natural events as teaching opportunities. Your child may be ready to learn about events that she witnesses such as your telling a "white lie" or bending the rules of a game so a small child can win. Some events that occur can be used to enrich your child's understanding of the complexities of social interaction.

Summary

Perspective taking is a skill requiring that we understand how another person is experiencing or feeling about something. It is the foundation of many of our social connections, as it helps us to plan our social initiations and to respond to others. Perspective taking is a formidable challenge for children with autism. It may be best to begin by working on activities that involve concrete objects (such as the physical orientation activities), before addressing the social and emotional manifestations of this concept.

A variety of related skills will help your child to understand people's expectations regarding objects and situations. These skills will help your child to make hypotheses about what someone would think or expect in a given situation. It is also important for your child to understand the motivation behind providing false information or cheating. This will help your child to recognize the complexity of social interactions, and may help insulate her from unfair practices by others. Finally, your child will be more successful as a friend if she can show compassion and understanding toward others. The development of empathy is an important social task that represents the highest achievement in understanding the perspective of another person.

References

Baron-Cohen, S., Leslie, A. M. & Frith, U. (1985). Does the autistic child have a "theory of mind"? *Cognition, 21,* 37-46.

Gray, C., & Garand, J. (1993). Social stories: Improving responses of students with autism with accurate social information. *Focus on Autistic Behavior, 8,* 1-10.

Happe, F. (1995). *Autism: An introduction to psychological theory.* Cambridge, MA: Harvard University Press.

Hobson, R. P. (1993). Autism and the development of mind. Mahwah, New Jersey: Lawrence Erlbaum Associates.

Hobson, R. P. (1986). The autistic child's appraisal of expression of emotion. *Journal of Child Psychology and Psychiatry, 27,* 321-42.

Lord, C. (1993). Early social development in autism. In E. Schopler, M. E. van Bourgondien, and M. M. Bristol (Eds.), *Preschool issues in autism.* New York, NY: Plenum Press.

5 | Starting School

Scott Kimball Starts a Preschool Program

Over the course of sixteen months, Scott Kimball made excellent progress in his home-based ABA program. His cognitive skills and his speech showed steady growth and he was much more socially aware than he had been when the program began. As part of Scott's preparation for moving into a preschool program, he was spending more time with other children.

Initially Scott's sister, Rita, was his only playmate. Their interactions began with simple toy play and gradually evolved into more complex games. Once Scott could play with Rita, his parents invited the boy who lived next door to be a playmate for Scott. With a bit of coaching, this boy, who was seven years old and very patient with younger children, was able to engage Scott in the same games that Scott and Rita enjoyed.

Gradually, over the next few months, they invited other children, including some preschool-age children, to become playmates. Scott reached the point where he could be part of a group of four or five children, playing with one or two of them at a time, and going along with the whole group when an adult led them in an activity. He was also going to Saturday morning gym class at the local YMCA, where, with a little coaching from his father, he kept up with the other children.

Matt Becker suggested to the Kimballs that it was time to introduce Scott to a preschool class. His school readiness skills, such as following directions, sitting quietly, and engaging in some social play, now came close to his age level and his social skills were sufficient to get along in a group.

The plan was to start with an hour of school a day for two or three days a week, then slowly increase the time once Scott was ready to tolerate more contact with the other children. Scott would attend school with an adult who would be his "shadow" (coach) and would intervene if he got into serious trouble such as having tantrums or feeling bewildered about what to do next. At first, the shadow would stick close to Scott so that she could intervene whenever needed. Over time, she would move farther away and work with Scott within a group of children, and as much as possible, not intrude into Scott's day. The shadow would work closely with the teacher and support the teacher's effort.

Matt explained that a shadow is not intended to act as a one-to-one teacher for the child with autism. Rather, she supports him in being part of a group of children who attend to and respond to the teacher's directions.

Matt emphasized to Allison and Jack that the most crucial component of this arrangement would be a receptive classroom teacher. He encouraged them to visit several schools and look for a teacher who provided a fair amount of structure for the class, including clear rules. She should also offer a great deal of reinforcement for appropriate behavior. If they could find a teacher who already had experience including children with various disabilities, it might be a sign that she was receptive to working with a variety of needs. The teacher would also have to be willing to accept a shadow in the classroom. Furthermore, she would have to be willing to alter her strategies for instruction and for reinforcement, and might need to use an incentive system developed just for Scott.

Is Your Child Ready for an Inclusion Experience?

Scott made rapid progress in his home-based program and was ready for an inclusion experience after sixteen months. However, many children need considerably more time at home or in a center-based program before they have all of the prerequisite skills.

Scott had mastered many programs in a variety of domains. These included very substantial progress in his pre-kindergarten readiness skills such as matching, sorting, picture identification, and number concepts. He also made steady social progress and was aware of and interested in other children. Although he was still not very "smooth" in his social approaches, he did invite other children to play and participated in a variety of childhood games. He could work with a small group of children for short periods of time and follow group directions. He had no serious behavior problems, was not aggressive with other children, and could be redirected when he had one of his brief tantrums.

Different school systems have different ideas about when to include a child with autism in a regular education class. Some might include a child who still needs mostly one-to-one instruction all day and who shows little awareness of other people. Other school systems might think that this same youngster still needs the intensity of education that can only be provided in a specialized setting. Our own perspective is to advocate for inclusion when:

1. a child is able to learn in a group,
2. he shows an awareness of other children, and
3. he rarely if ever engages in behavior that might upset classmates.

Although some professionals might argue to include every child with autism in a typical classroom, we are more concerned about ensuring that children get the intensity of instruction needed to build skills than about providing sheer proximity to peers. At this point, however, there is little research to guide these decisions about inclusion.

In our opinion, some children with autism need a blend of time in an inclusive classroom and time in a special education setting or resource room. It is not uncommon for a child who is included for much of the day to spend some time in a resource room, working on subjects where he requires additional support. We are strong advocates of flexibility on behalf of children. The best possible combination of inclusion and support should be crafted for each child based on his needs.

In this chapter, we discuss some guidelines to follow in deciding when and how to arrange an inclusion experience for your child. We also discuss the roles of the shadow, the classroom teacher, and the teaching team as a whole. We describe skills a child needs before he enters the classroom and skills that need to be taught early in his transition to the classroom. Finally, we consider how to take advantage of the programming opportunities that are available in an inclusive class.

What Is an Inclusive Classroom?

There are different words used to describe classrooms in which children with autism are educated alongside of typically developing peers. Among the terms to describe these settings are "inclusive," mainstreamed," and "integrated."

The phrase "integrated class" is often used to refer to a special education class that includes typically developing peer models among its students. For example, at the Douglass School, our Small Wonders preschool class has both children with autism and their typical peers in the same room.

In contrast to the term "integrated," the word "mainstreamed" is often used to describe a regular education class that includes one or more children with special needs. These classes have a majority of typically developing children and perhaps one to four children with disabilities. A child with autism who is placed in a regular kindergarten would be described as in a mainstream class or perhaps as "mainstreamed." Some people also use the term "mainstreamed" to mean that a child with disabilities is in a typical class without support.

The term "inclusion" may be the best one to use for general discussion because it refers to any situation in which children with autism or other disabilities are brought together with their peers. It is helpful to know that different professionals use the terms integrated, mainstreamed, and included differently. You should check on the makeup of the classroom in which your child could be placed and not assume that your understanding of these terms is the same as the school personnel's.

Academic Benefits of Inclusion

Children with autism learn many basic cognitive skills in one-to-one home-based or center-based teaching. However, if they are to function in a regular classroom, it is essential that they be able to transfer these pre-academic skills to a classroom setting. They must also be able to learn in a group, as well as with the individual teaching that was the focus of their early instruction.

Many children with autism are unable to learn in a group when they enter treatment. It may take time for your child to achieve that goal, and some children with autism are never able to function independently in a group. For those children who have the ability to do so, however, it is important that they learn to be part of the class. Learning through group instruction is essential to being able to function well in a typical class.

For the preschool-age child, group instruction skills mean sitting quietly in a circle, responding by raising your hand when the teacher asks a question, following directions for group activities, and participating in discussions about such topics as the weather, the day and date of the week, and so forth. The kindergarten child will use all of these skills and more as he is introduced to more advanced pre-academic skills such as number and letter recognition and individual work sheets. For the first grade child, there is the added expectation of doing independent seatwork.

These kinds of classroom behaviors can be shaped by having your child gradually move from individual work to work with one other child, then two children, and on up to the size of class in your community. You can also fade the additional support your child needs within the classroom itself. For example, at first he may be allowed to leave the circle after five minutes, then ten minutes, and so on.

Social Benefits of Inclusion

A primary advantage of inclusive classrooms is the enhanced opportunity to teach social skills to the child with autism. Typically developing peers provide role models and are often responsive partners for the social initiations of the child with autism. Although some social skills training can be done in special education classes composed exclusively of children with autism, the lack of appropriate models and the relative lack of responsiveness among classmates limits what can be mastered in that specialized setting.

Research and classroom practice have shown that children with autism can learn a variety of social skills in the classroom, including:

- ◆ playing games,
- ◆ expressing affection,
- ◆ fantasy play, and
- ◆ assertiveness in play and conversation.

One important conclusion from this research is that it is usually not a good idea for the teacher or shadow to be the primary source of reinforcement for appropriate social behavior. If we want children to enjoy playing with one another, they must serve as the main source of reinforcement for one another. If the teacher intervenes too much, we run the risk that in her absence the child with autism will not use social behaviors such as approaching other children or responding to their attempts at interaction.

It is also important for your child with autism to learn to initiate social interactions with his peers. In research where the peers learned to approach the child with autism, but not vice versa, the child with autism remained dependent on peer initiation to become engaged in play. He did not learn that sometimes he must take the first step to play with another child. If he remains dependent on assertive peers, he will not know what to do when other children do not ask him to play with them.

The most effective settings for learning social skills are those that combine a creative, supportive teacher, responsive, cooperative peers, and children with autism who are trained in how to initiate play. Early in the teaching of social skills, a teacher may need to "prime the pump" by encouraging the children's efforts to play together. To do this, she should select peers who are friendly and cooperative and also be certain that any child who does not want to play with the child with autism is not forced to do so. She may, for example, suggest to a peer that he ask a classmate with autism to play and encourage him to be persistent if the classmate does not respond right away. Without initial adult support, the typically developing peer may be discouraged by the lack of interest from the child with autism. If one peer becomes overly protective of the child with autism, that youngster can be encouraged to let the child with autism "try it himself."

Similarly, the teacher initially may coach the child with autism in how to approach another child in the class and start a game. Over time, the teacher will withdraw this support and allow the natural pleasure of play to become a primary reward for the children's play.

Psychologist Catherine Lord (1993) has suggestions for enhancing the social inclusion of the child with autism. As shown in Table 5-1, one of these guidelines is to make sure the toys and activities that are available to the children are very attractive. Be certain that the things the children can do together are appealing. Also be certain they are not too complicated for the child with autism to master. For example, dress-up clothes, doll houses, play airports, attractive building blocks, and make-believe grocery stores would all be of interest to many children, allow for roles that differed in complexity, and encourage interaction.

Table 5-1 | Some Guidelines for Inclusion

- Use attractive toys and activities.
- Make sure activities are within abilities of children.
- Organize around themes.
- Choose activities that are not too long.

Classroom Activities

Lord suggests that class themes can help the teacher organize the class around interesting topics. For example, during a month spent on "community helpers," there could be firefighter helmets, physician's jackets, and police officer's gear available for play, along with fire trucks, garbage trucks, and toy ambulances. Other topics for classroom themes include holidays, pets, and questions such as "what lives in the water" or "how do flowers grow."

It is important to remember that young children have relatively brief attention spans. Very young children may not be able to tolerate more than five to ten minutes on a single activity, while older children may enjoy a half-hour of sustained play around a single theme. Younger children will also need more help shifting from one task to another, while older children may move among activities with minimal adult intervention.

Skills for Peers

There are some specific skills peers can learn in order to be supportive of their classmate with autism. One of these is being persistent in their efforts to engage the child with autism. Peers should be encouraged to "try again" and not be easily discouraged. Another skill is to join the child with autism in an activity that he seems to be enjoying. Initially the teacher might suggest that the peer "Play blocks with Rick," when she spots the child with autism playing alone. Later, she might make a quiet comment to reward that effort. All of the children in the classroom, with and without autism, should be taught to call the teacher if they have a problem with another child.

Peers may need help understanding the special needs of the child with autism. For example, if your child has a hard time tolerating people who get too close, the peers may need to learn to respect boundaries. Young children may need very concrete guidelines such as, "If you can reach out and touch him, you're too close." Meanwhile, your child with autism may need to be taught to approach closer than he has in the past. Similarly, if your child with autism has auditory processing problems, his classmates may learn to "give him time" to respond before they jump in to do things for him.

It is important to consider ahead of time whether you want your child's classmates to know that he has any special problems. You should discuss this with the educational team and be certain everyone will support your decision. Children with autism vary tremendously in their characteristics and abilities. Many children leaving intensive ABA programs are virtually indistinguishable from their peers. In this case, you may decide that there is no need to educate or train peers, and that you do not want your child's diagnosis or difficulties to be a topic of discussion with his classmates.

Even if your child has behaviors or characteristics that set him apart from his peers, you may prefer that information about your child not be shared with his peers. Or perhaps you may not want the teacher to use the label "autism," but may feel comfortable with having peers know that your child has trouble talking or sometimes needs to sit in a quiet place for a few minutes. The strategies discussed above can be used with peers whether or not the peers are informed of your child's diagnosis or difficulties.

Skills for the Child with Autism

Not every peer in the community will have the benefit of training that will make him a good role model or supportive partner for

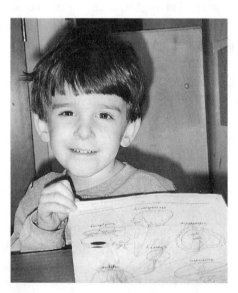

your child with autism. It is therefore essential that your child master the skills to initiate and sustain social interactions with other children. Ideally he would do this before he became part of the class so that his "differences" would be less obvious to his classmates. Once he has learned these skills, he can approach other children and play with them and is not dependent on the other child or on the prompting of a teacher or a shadow. As we described earlier in this book, your child also needs to know the essential skills for manipulating toys and for the pretend play of childhood.

Before being expected to spend extended amounts of time with other youngsters, your child should be engaging in only a minimal number of aggressive or disruptive behaviors. Children are understandably afraid of the child who hits them, has long, loud tantrums, or in other ways behaves very inappropriately in the classroom. In addition, it is best if your child's behavior can be managed with techniques similar to those used for other students in the classroom.

Verbal feedback and reprimands are the most frequent methods of correction in a class. When these do not work, one common discipline method is a brief time-out, during which your child must remain in a chair and watch while the other children play. Another consequence for misbehavior might be to withhold the tokens, stars, points, or other symbols that are awarded to children for good behavior and which are later "cashed in" for treats. Certain privileges might also be lost as a result of misbehavior, such as choice of dessert at lunch or extra time on the playground. However, in using these methods, remember that time-out only works if your child does not find the experience an enjoyable one that allows him to engage in self-stimulatory behavior or escape from work, and an incentive system is only potent if the reinforcements are personally motivating to your child. If your child does not like sweets, he is not likely to work very hard to earn them!

Selecting a Classroom for Inclusion

If you are able to choose among two or more classrooms for your child, visit each and watch the teacher. Does he have clear rules for the children to follow? For example, do they know what to do when they need help or have finished their work?

Are there good cues to signal the children to change activities? Many teachers will ring a bell, turn off the lights, clap hands, or use some other signal to indicate to the children that it is time to pay attention. Does the teacher praise the children for good behavior? A teacher who gives young children liberal doses of praise or uses a token system in class would be a good match for the child with autism.

When you talk to the teacher, does he seem open to at least modest accommodations (modifications to the typical school environment), such as changing where your child's desk is located or using a simple token system? Does he appear open to your input? If the teacher announces very firmly that this is the way she always has and always will run his class, he may lack the flexibility to adapt to your child. As we discuss in the next section, many children with autism need the support of an adult coach (shadow) during the transition to a typical class. Will the teacher accept a shadow in the classroom? If the teacher can't work with a shadow, the placement may not work well.

If this is a public school placement as opposed to a preschool class, you should also talk to the principal and a member of the child study team to assess how supportive they will be of you, your child, and of the teacher. The child study team (sometimes called a Pupil Evaluation Team or Administrative Placement Committee) is a group of educational professionals who are responsible for evaluating your child and assessing his progress. This team will often include a school psychologist, a speech and language specialist, a social worker, and a teacher. You as a parent are also legally part of the team. Other specialists, such as a physician, physical therapist, or occupational therapist, may also serve, depending on your child's needs. These professionals can be a valuable resource.

A school might not have all of the ideal characteristics you have hoped for, but one where the staff members seem open to your input, willing to think of your child's specific needs, and flexible in making accommodations should create a sufficient level of support to make inclusion work.

Becoming a Good Team

If the transition from a home-based or center-based program to a typical classroom is to go smoothly, the adults involved must understand their roles and work well with one another. Several people have key roles in making the transition effective. First, there is your role as a parent. You are a member of the child study team for your child and his most devoted advocate. The teacher in charge of the classroom also plays a central role in inclusion. In addition, a person assigned to work directly with your child should probably support the teacher in her efforts. Many people use the term "shadow" for this individual. You might also hear the terms "classroom aide," "para-professional," or "one-on-one aide" used to describe this person. It is function and not title that matters.

Other school personnel, including a resource room teacher, speech-language pathologist, and school psychologist may play a role in the inclusion process. If the school psychologist does not have in-depth expertise in the use of applied behavior analysis in an inclusive setting, you will also need an ABA consultant who can guide the team in its work. With so many different people playing a role, it is very important that a cohesive team is created and that everyone works well together toward their common goal of enabling your child to be successful in the classroom.

The Parents' Role

Building good communication takes active listening in which participants attend to the speaker rather than just waiting their turn to speak. Each of the team members needs to understand and be respectful of the stress involved in the role of others. For example, this transition is an inherently stressful one for parents. If your child has been in a home-based program, you will have become accustomed to having total control over your child's instruction. Although that role is demanding, it is also empowering and some parents find it hard to give up that level of control when their child enters a typical class. It becomes the parents' role to surrender some control to the teaching staff.

The Teachers' Role

For their part, the teachers need to respect the stress involved in this change, and recognize the need to keep parents well informed. Some teachers, especially those who are relatively inexperienced, may be uncomfortable working with parents who have more experience than they do in using the methods of applied behavior analysis. The wise parent recognizes the discomfort the teacher faces in this situation and works to minimize that tension by conveying respect for the teacher and her accomplishments. You can also help each other. While you may be more adept at creating task analyses or token systems, she will be an invaluable resource on academic instructional strategies for critical skills.

The teacher is responsible for the entire classroom and has multiple demands on her time. Your child with autism is one child in a class that will include other children who also need her attention. If the shadow or the parents fail to recognize these multiple demands, they may have unrealistic expectations and estrange a teacher who entered the relationship hoping to be helpful. The teacher, for her part, needs to be clear about the expectations for her classroom and areas in which she believes she can or cannot make adjustments.

One challenge to working well as a team is that the classroom teacher may not be familiar with the use of applied behavior analysis. She may have a commitment to a different approach to managing her classroom and it may require some give and take to work out an approach that meets her needs as well as your child's needs. This may be simply a matter of using different vocabularies or it may reflect more substantial differences in approach. In resolving these differences, it is helpful to remain focused on the needs of your child. It is important for all of the team members to be patient and hear each other's views. It is also important to be flexible and open to new ideas and strategies. When they advocate for a solution, the team members should provide reasons and data.

We have found that when school personnel want more information about applied behavior analysis and discrete trial instruction, they should be offered a simple overview rather than a research paper filled with technical terminology. One such resource is our book, *Right from the Start: Behavioral Intervention for Young Children with Autism* (Woodbine House, 1998). Another resource is the book edited by psychologist Michael Powers, *Children with Autism: A Parents' Guide* (Woodbine House, 2000). It should be made clear, however, that the information they receive in this context is an introduction to a complex methodology. Those who want more can then follow up in depth.

The teacher will want clarity about the role of the shadow and how the two of them are to interact. For example, they need to agree on who is to deal with behavior problems, who will prompt your child to respond, who will intervene if your child needs help, and who is to be the contact with your family. These roles may change over time and it is important that both the teacher and the shadow deliver rewards and redirect misbehavior. An early meeting between the shadow and the teacher before there are children in the classroom and insistent demands on the teacher's attention may be a good way to lay the groundwork for their relationship.

The shadow should also meet other staff members who will interact with your child, such as the speech-language pathologist and physical education teacher. If there is a resource room teacher involved, the shadow and resource teacher can discuss how their time will be spent when they are both in the room. One possibility is that the shadow can compile data or prepare materials while the resource teacher works with your child.

The Shadow's Role

The shadow's role is also a complex one. Frequently shadows have had previous experience with the child with autism

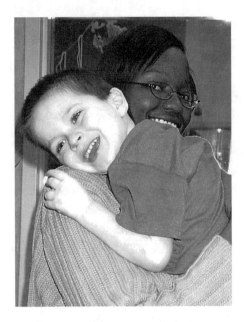

and have developed a caring relationship with him. Usually the shadow will have worked with the child in an intensive program, often at home. As a result, he or she has a tremendous amount of experience with the child and knowledge of the child. This puts them in an excellent situation to facilitate the child's transition into an integrated educational setting. They know all of the child's behavioral nuances, including subtle signs that he may be overwhelmed or unsure of the expectations of the task. They also know which skills the child has mastered, with what materials, and with what instructions. They know the extent to which the child has generalized a particular skill. They know which prompts the child generally responds to, and which rewards really result in good performance.

The shadow's knowledge about your child can be an immense asset to the entire educational team. It increases efficiency at the beginning of the year, as one team member already has a tremendous amount of knowledge of and familiarity with the child. Many of the staff members, children, and parents who come in contact with your child will know little about autism, applied behavior analysis, or about your child. It can smooth the process if they are given some fundamental information. Your child's shadow can play a key role in helping school staff understand your child and his special needs.

The shadow can help the classroom staff understand that the techniques that are effective with typical peers may not be effective for children with autism. He or she can familiarize the staff with procedures that have been helpful for your child in the past. Staff members also need to be made aware of how the symptoms of autism influence a child's behavior and learning patterns. This understanding may help them understand the challenges your child faces and the need to make special accommodations to these challenges. It will also help them to develop strategies for presenting materials, rewarding effort, and managing challenging behaviors.

While all of these skills make the shadow an ideal person to facilitate your child's transition, they also complicate the role. The shadow may feel quite protective of your child and want to remain his primary contact person in the classroom. Your child may come to depend on the shadow and resist the efforts of other adults to take over the instruction. In fact, the problems in generalization shown by children with autism make it likely that initially they will not take directions from the teacher as well as they do from a familiar shadow.

Their prior relationship with the parents may make it difficult for shadows to recognize that they have now become partners with the teacher, as well as the family. In addition, shadows often do not have as much formal education as teachers and may feel uncomfortable around the teacher because of this. Transferring from a home-based program into the school setting changes the shadow's relationship with the family. While it is important to involve the family in all decisions, it may not be appropriate for the shadow to discuss all school issues with the parents. This is especially true of issues that do not involve their child. It is important to acknowledge and respect the collegial nature of the relationships with other school staff. It is also important to allow the parents, rather than the shadow, to advocate for the child, although the shadow can certainly convey concerns to the parents.

In general, a familiar and trained person makes the best shadow for a child with autism and parents should advocate for that, if possible. When a familiar person is not feasible, parents should find out if the school will allow them to take part in the process of interviewing and selecting the shadow. Some school districts will allow this and others will not. Sometimes a school district will suggest that a classroom aide can serve the purpose of a shadow while also attending to the needs of other children. Over time, your child may be fine with this level of support, but at first he will likely need one-to-one attention.

When a shadow who has no prior experience is hired, training is essential. Training should take place prior to the school year, and should also be ongoing. Depending on the school's resources, this training might be done by a member of the child study team, an experienced teacher, or by an outside consultant in applied behavior analysis, perhaps the same one who has worked with your child and family in preparing him to enter school. If the school system does not have an expert in applied behavior analysis on the staff, you will want to be certain that you address that problem in your child's IEP (individualized education program). For example, it can be written into the IEP that an expert in ABA will be consulted for staff training, as well as for managing behavior problems and instructional problems that may arise over the course of the year. Anything written into the IEP is the financial responsibility of the school district.

As part of the shadow's preparation, it may be possible to have the individual meet and spend time with your child. He or she may even observe several sessions at home, or you may be able to do several sessions at school with a familiar staff member, while the shadow observes. Any arrangement that helps your child and his shadow get to know one another will help to ease the transition to school.

In sum, each of the players comes to the table with some concerns and worries. To the extent that they can treat one another with respect and openness, the process of integrating your child with autism into the classroom will go smoothly. Talking about concerns and looking for solutions in which everyone (especially your child) is a winner will go a long way toward building an effective team.

Essential Skills for Team Members

Skills for Parents. Parents of a child with autism in an included setting have a central role in making the placement work. You should continue to work with your child at home, building his skills in the natural environment and ensuring that programming efforts between home and school are consistent. In addition, no matter how splendid your child's team is, you need to be an effective advocate for your child. This means expressing concerns and working constructively toward solutions. It also means recognizing the achievements of the school team and finding ways to regularly acknowledge their efforts. Don't forget the importance of letting people know what they are doing right as well as ways in which they might improve their effort. Don't assume that because "they get paid to do their job," teachers do not need your respect and appreciation. We all need that!

Skills for Shadows. You may want to specify the skills of the shadow in your child's IEP. The shadow should be well trained in behavioral teaching methods. He should know how to fade his presence so he becomes less and less central to your child's performance, when to prompt a response, how to fade prompts, how to provide just enough subtle guidance, how to collect data, and so forth.

The shadow must understand that the teacher is in charge of the classroom and be able to relate well to her as the teacher. Different school systems appoint a variety of people to act as the shadow's supervisor; that person should have regular contact with the shadow and provide coaching for the shadow in how to establish good working relationships in the school.

In addition, some teachers may want all of the family contact about the child to go through them as teacher, while others may be comfortable sharing this role with the shadow. In our opinion, it works best when both the shadow and the teacher communicate with the family. They should also share this correspondence with one another. This contact can include phone calls, a daily written log that goes back and forth between home and school, and face-to-face meetings. The shadow who has a role in family communication needs to understand the importance of remaining closely coordinated with the teacher.

Skills for Teachers. Inclusion works best when the teacher is well trained for the experience and feels confident in her skills. A teacher who resents the placement of children with autism in her class, who has a class so large she cannot manage it, or who does not have the necessary technical skills in applied behavior analysis is not likely to create an effective opportunity for the child with autism.

The teacher should have the support of a well-trained shadow who can assume primary responsibility for the child with autism when necessary. The teacher should understand the fundamentals of applied behavior analysis, including the use of prompts, fading of prompts, the use of reinforcement, and so forth. There are a number of ways to get this training. Some of it can be done "hands on" from a consultant who is knowledgeable about applied behavior analysis and who comes to the classroom to work with the teacher. This person might be a member of the child study team or someone from outside the school system who works with schools who need help implementing programs for children with autism. There are also college courses in applied behavior analysis and workshops offered by various professional groups for teachers who wish an introduction to these skills.

Easing the Transition Into a Typical Class

Although a well-trained school staff is essential if your child is going to do well in an inclusive setting, it is equally important that your child with autism come to the classroom with basic skills that will allow him to function in that setting.

As a first step in helping your child move into a typical classroom, it is important to maximize the similarities between what you are doing at home or in a center-based program and what is done in the typical classroom. For example, a classroom teacher may use different words for directions than your child heard at home. Your child can be taught these new phrases by pairing them with familiar wording. This can be targeted at home or at the center during generalization training. The shadow could also help your child learn the terms, as could the speech-language pathologist. For example, you could pair the new instruction (e.g., "where does this belong?") with the one that is familiar to your child (e.g., "put with same"). Over time, you would fade the pairing.

Another adjustment to prepare your child for is the change from discrete trial instruction to regular classroom instruction. Children with autism are often accustomed to short trials and numerous short breaks. In school, children are expected to sit for longer periods with fewer breaks. Setting time goals during home programming or in your child's center-based program is a good way to ease this change.

The first step is to determine your child's current capacity for focusing his attention on learning so you can set a sensible starting point. For example, if the current time span is five minutes, he gets a reward such as a token, candy, or a drink of water at the end of this interval. Following the reward, he works for another five minutes to receive the next break or reward. During home- or center-based instruction, the length of this interval needs to be systematically increased over time. It may be helpful to use sight words such as "listen" to redirect your child. The word "listen" or a symbol for it can be written on a card and placed on your child's desk; if need be, the shadow can point toward it with her finger. This is often less intrusive than verbal redirections. Always remember to provide reinforcement for appropriate behavior and for compliance with requests or redirection

Consistency is crucial during the early stages of the transition. Some of the teaching methods used at home or in a center-based program may be very helpful in acclimating your child to the new setting. The classroom teacher will want to know how your child learned successfully in the past. For example, a list of familiar instructions may help the teacher pair unfamiliar classroom instructions with familiar ones from previous learning.

Likewise, the use of discrete trial instruction may be useful in the first days in the classroom if there is a good collaboration between teacher and shadow. For example, the teacher can ask your child a question, wait for him to answer, and praise him if he responds. If he gives a wrong answer, the teacher would follow the protocol for errors within your child's instructional program. This protocol might be to ignore the incorrect response, to give your child feedback that he is wrong, or to instruct your child in what the correct answer would be. The teacher can learn from the consultant in applied behavior analysis what method of discrete trial instruction is used with your child. While using discrete trial methods may feel awkward to the classroom teacher at first, it can serve as a useful bridge for your child and the format gets easier with practice.

We do not advocate the long-term use of discrete trial instruction in an inclusive setting. Instead, we ensure that the child is ready to move beyond discrete trial teaching when he enters an inclusive classroom. Even if your child is still receiving discrete trial instruction when he enters a classroom, it would typically be done outside of the inclusive setting. DTI is done more effectively in a less distracting setting and your child will feel less stigmatized if he is working in private.

Helping Your Child Generalize Skills

As discussed throughout this book, generalization of skills is challenging for children with autism. Not everything a child has learned at home will generalize immediately to the classroom. But, he will find it easier to transfer skills that he has been using consistently over a period of time and has learned to use in many different places such as at home, in the grocery store, and in a restaurant. Creating that backdrop for effective generalization is part of a parent's role in preparing their child for inclusion.

An important skill for functioning independently in the classroom is responding to instruction from the classroom teacher. As a parent, there are things you can do to help this happen. One is to be sure that the teacher knows your child's abilities in both academic areas and social skills. It is important to share his strengths as well as his weaknesses. For example, if he excels in math, the teacher can make an effort to call on him during math activities. This may help classmates recognize that your child has genuine strengths and abilities, as well as challenges. Areas of difficulty must also be conveyed to the teacher. Although the teacher may be reluctant to "push" your child excessively, he needs to learn that the rules at home also apply in school. He needs to see that the same or similar expectations will be required at school. Close communication between the teacher and the shadow can help to ensure that expectations are appropriate and consistent.

The communication between home and school can be boosted by a home-school communication log, filled out by both the teacher and the shadow at school and the parents at home. This log travels back and forth each day with the child. It is a place to share observations, concerns, achievements, and plans. If your child slept poorly the night before or if he ate poorly in school, this information can be noted in the log, as can facts about his academic and social performance. We also like to exchange data sheets with parents on a daily or weekly basis in order to track progress on our identified goals.

For some children, an obstacle to generalization in the classroom may be the teacher's lack of experience in how hard to press him to respond. Your child has learned over months and months of teaching that when you give him an instruction, he is expected to follow it. When the classroom teacher encounters noncompliance from your child, however, she may be reluctant to press him. The problem with this is that if your child's noncompliance is motivated even in part by an effort to escape from the task, the teacher's reluctance may unintentionally reinforce noncompliance.

This is a time when the shadow can help by assisting the teacher set expectations that are realistic and achievable. If your child knows the material, the shadow can help the teacher maintain appropriate expectations. If your child is struggling, the team must analyze and identify the source of difficulty. If your child truly does not understand the material, it may be necessary to modify the assignment, while still requiring him to complete the task. If he is having trouble staying on task, it may be possible to institute short breaks, although at some point he must return to the task and finish it.

The close link between home and school in problem solving is illustrated by our work with Ronnie. As shown in the shaded box on pages 194 and 195, Ronnie was able to benefit from home-based teaching that aimed at boosting her classroom skills. In this case video modeling was used to good effect for a little girl who had strong skills in generalization, but was having trouble learning how to learn in a group. This case illustrates nicely how different methods may be effective at one point in a child's learning, but not at another. We need to be flexible and creative in using the teaching technology of applied behavior analysis.

Increasing Your Child's Ability to Respond to the Classroom Teacher

Initially, your child may only respond to the shadow and then just to the teacher when he is being spoken to directly. Once he can attend when the teacher directs an instruction directly to him, your child needs to attend when the teacher gives directions to the class as a whole. As soon as it is feasible, the shadow should fade her role from one of intervening directly with your child to one of holding back unless needed. How long this takes will depend on your child's needs and the structure of the class, but it is a crucial goal for your child to attend to the teacher, not the shadow.

Your child may be more familiar with the shadow because he knows her from home or has more close interaction with her. As a result, he may pay more attention to the shadow than to the teacher. This highlights the need for clear and separate roles for the teacher and the shadow and is a problem they can address together. The shadow will need to redirect your child toward the teacher—for example, by using gestures or written prompts, and the teacher must make an effort to ensure that your child is attending to her when she gives instructions. To get your child's attention, the teacher might stand close to his desk and be sure she has eye contact when she gives directions.

Some children with autism who responded very well to their individual instruction in the preschool years may not need a full-time shadow when they start kindergarten. These children may still need extra teacher attention, and may benefit from being seated close to the teacher's desk, having the teacher deliberately get their attention when giving class directions, being provided with some extra structure, and a good motivational system.

Just as you kept regular records on your child's learning at home, you will want to track what he learns in school. It is a good idea to assess how much your child is learning when he sits quietly in class and appears to attend to the teacher. When the teacher introduces a new concept in class, it might be appropriate to do a pretest before the concept is taught to the class and then after to see whether your child is absorbing information through this group format. The shadow may be the person to do this assessment.

If your child does not appear to be learning, you need to do a closer assessment of the factors that are involved. Is it the material being taught? The way it is being taught? Your child's motivation to perform? For example, if he can learn the material readily with one-to-one instruction, then it is probably not the material per se. In this case, perhaps increasing his motivation by providing more reinforcement in the classroom would make a difference. He may also need more assistance from the shadow if the shift to group learning has been too rapid.

Children with autism often have problems in school because they don't know how to monitor or understand the subtle non-verbal gestures of the teacher and other children. These include gestures indicating that it is time to be quiet, to sit down, or to lower voices. An important part of the shadow's responsibility is to identify the non-verbal cues used in the classroom and throughout the school. These cues need to be systematically taught to your child by the shadow, the parents, or the teacher. At first, these silent cues may need to be paired with verbal or written instructions.

> ## Ronnie Learns How to Learn in a Group
>
> Ronnie had done exceptionally well in her home-based ABA program, where her rate of learning in one-to-one teaching was very rapid, and she mastered multiple new items in a single day. Even more impressively, she generalized (transferred) that knowledge with relative ease. In spite of this impressive strength, she had trouble integrating into school.
>
> Initially, her ability to generalize made the transition to school fairly easy. Ronnie responded easily to her teacher's directions, even when they were worded in novel and unfamiliar ways. She had no difficulty working with the materials in the classroom, and she displayed her skills with apparent ease. During the early weeks, when Ronnie was new to the classroom, her instructional assistant stayed close by. After a while, the assistant reduced her attention during work activities. Even with less supervision, Ronnie stayed on task and completed her assignments independently.
>
> In spite of this fine individual work, Ronnie had difficulty learning during group instruction. She didn't attend well in a group and was often not able to answer the teacher in this context. At first, Ronnie's parents thought she just needed more practice. They arranged at home for more analog circle times and story times with children in the neighborhood. When this didn't work, they wrote social stories and rule cards about correct group behavior. They practiced role plays about sitting and attending in a group. None of these efforts seemed to make a difference. The reports Ronnie brought home from school remained unchanged. Group time was still a struggle for her, and she didn't appear to be learning from group lessons.
>
> At this point, Ronnie's parents turned to their ABA consultant for help. He determined that one problem was Ronnie's physical over-activity; she was constantly fidgeting during group lessons. Not only was this likely contributing to her inattention, it also seemed to

Increasing Your Child's Independence in Following the School Schedule

Independence in the classroom is the ultimate goal of the integration process. Using effective prompts is key to building this capacity for independent work. To support this goal, the shadow should be consistently assessing and refining the level of irritate her teacher and her peers. Furthermore, Ronnie failed to make eye contact with the teacher and with the other main speakers within the group. As a result, she seemed to be "missing" the content of the lessons.

The team was concerned that Ronnie wasn't getting enough practice with group skills at school. They also knew that the analog practice at home was ineffective. To provide more practice, they videotaped regular group instructional lessons at school. Ronnie watched these lessons at home, while her parents prompted her to sit still and attend to the teacher. Through a token system, she received concrete rewards for displaying attentive behavior. Ronnie's attentiveness improved quickly while watching the tapes at home.

Over time, Ronnie's parents faded (reduced) their assistance to Ronnie while she watched the tapes, and she was able to independently practice "circle time" and other group lessons at home. The token system was then extended into school, where it was needed only briefly before it was faded. Ronnie was able to attend to group lessons much more successfully.

One incidental teaching strategy used during the video practice was peer modeling. Ronnie's parents would often point out how her friend Joan was behaving. Ronnie began emulating Joan's behavior, both while watching the tape and in the classroom.

Even with all of the success of the videotapes, certain group instructional times were still a challenge for Ronnie. For example, during arts and crafts, her attention would drift. Her parents addressed this issue through the use of rule cards to remind her of the importance of paying attention. Interestingly, this strategy had failed prior to the videotape practice sessions. It may be that Ronnie simply needed more practice with the concepts. Or, it may be that the videotaped lessons were a much closer "analog" than the previous practice sessions. In any case, using the videotaped lessons from school made the rule cards more effective.

assistance your child needs, and determining the times and routines in which he is independent.

Look for every opportunity to evaluate how much of a prompt is needed for an activity and be ready to step aside and allow your child to proceed on his own whenever possible. For example, in the beginning your child might need continual verbal direction to learn the morning routine in the classroom. Then these

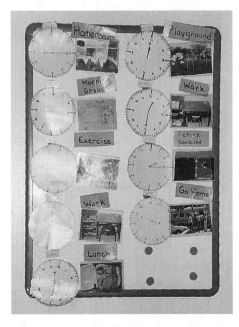

verbal prompts might be faded to picture or word cards. For example, the verbal cue "Go to your desk" might be paired with a picture of a desk. Then the spoken words might be faded by saying only "Go" and showing the picture. Eventually, this cue may be faded out one picture or line of text at a time, until all special prompts are gone.

Independence also includes your child's ability to take direction from the classroom teacher rather than the shadow, begin work on his own, and initiate interactions with his peers. It may occasionally be necessary to let your child perform tasks without prompts and stumble, in order to see exactly what level of assistance is needed. When fading of a prompt is premature, you can always return to the previous level of assistance.

The Power of Imitation and Learning by Watching

As mentioned before, the abundance of typical models is a major advantage of including children with autism in a typical classroom. Throughout this book we have described ways to encourage your child to learn by watching other children. We discussed ways to systematically teach him to do what another child or an adult is doing. When your child transfers to the typical classroom, this learning by watching is key.

The shadow plays an important role in helping your child use his observational learning skills in the classroom. When the other children are following the teacher's directions, the shadow will prompt your child to follow his peers. Learning to do that gives your child a strategy to use when he misses the teacher's directions. He can get cues from what his peers are doing. The shadow can redirect your child with the instruction, "Do what your friends are doing," or with the question, "What are your friends doing?"

Imitating other children is useful in other settings as well. For example, recess and gym are excellent opportunities to build peer imitation skills. Your child can be prompted to do what the other children do as they play together. Because these activities may be more intrinsically rewarding to children than work in the classroom, there is great potential for incidental learning. The better your child becomes at observational learning, the more he will have this skill available for use in many settings over the years. It is a skill we all rely upon every day to understand new experiences or master new skills.

Helping Your Child Get Along with Other Children

Another important thing children learn in school is how to get along with one another. Your child needs to learn these lessons as well, although the symptoms of his autism make this task more challenging than it is for other children. There are things parents, shadows, and teachers can do to support this new learning. One fundamental strategy is to encourage and reinforce all attempts made by your child to interact with his peers.

In the beginning, the responses of other children may not be intrinsically reinforcing to your child, so classroom staff may need tangible reinforcers such as tokens or stickers to support his effort. They may also have to set up special situations that encourage interaction. For example, the teacher may withhold a crayon when she passes out material so that your child has to ask a peer to borrow one. Similarly, she may arrange group activities where items must be shared (e.g., scissors or glue) and your child must request them. In the beginning, your child may

need a gestural or verbal prompt to approach classmates and request the material. A problem-solving approach might involve asking your child, "What do you need?" When he says, "crayon," the teacher or shadow can ask, "Who has one?" When your child names a peer, he can then be encouraged to ask that child for a crayon.

One good way to facilitate your child's social skills as well as academic skills is to involve him in activities with small numbers of peers who are models of appropriate behavior. It is important to identify activities that are natural opportunities for interaction. Examples might include a science project requiring a team of three; buddy reading; tutoring one another in spelling words, object labels, or letters; or having one child carry a box of materials while another puts items on the desks. During lunch and recess, the teacher or shadow can prompt your child with autism and other children to engage in conversations appropriate to their age on such topics as birthday parties, favorite cartoons, or sports. Fridays, Mondays, and holidays are perfect times to get children talking about their upcoming and recent experiences.

Daily classroom routines such as morning greetings can be used to promote your child's initiation skills. For example, it can be written into the IEP that your child is required to initiate greetings with two or three children daily. This allows for multiple trials in a natural setting and may or may not require any additional reinforcement beyond the exchange between the children.

During free play and recess, your child can ask other children to join him in a game. He may also ask peers if he can join in their game or activity. The peers are not, of course, required to join in the play, but your child should be encouraged to approach children who have shown themselves to be receptive. The shadow can help by suggesting familiar, enjoyable games for your child to propose to other children. Initiation of interactions can be one of the more daunting skills for children with autism, and parents, shadows, and teachers will need to look for opportunities to support this learning.

Preparing Your Child's Peers

How important it is to explain your child's needs to his peers in the classroom depends on how unusual his behavior is. Some children are demonstrating only subtle symptoms by the time they are included in a typical class, while others may have a variety of unusual behaviors. If your child is likely to engage in inappropriate or bizarre behavior, it is probably best to help the other children in the class understand something about autism.

One way to approach such a conversation would be for the teacher and shadow to talk with the children about all of the ways in which they and your child are alike. After some discussion of these similarities, it may be easy to move to the ways they differ. Depending on the conversation and the child, the youngster with autism might be part of this conversation or not. Ideally, if your child is present, the discussion should focus not just on him, but on helping all the children understand that we each have needs to be taken into consideration.

It is also important to help peers recognize that everyone has things that they do well and things that are hard for them. Peers can list what they do well and what they struggle with. Then the facilitator, who may be the shadow or the teacher, can share what things the child with autism does well and what things are hard for him.

If your child needs a great deal of help to function in the classroom, it will be important to explain the shadow's role to the children. However, for many children with autism, the shadow's role can be relatively subtle and there may be no need to link that person directly to the child with autism. The shadow may be just another helpful adult in the classroom. In other circumstances, it is best to say that the shadow is there primarily to help the child with autism. Children can be asked to tell the teacher or the shadow if there is a problem with the child with autism. If a behavioral problem occurs, peers will need reassurance that the shadow will take care of things.

For some children, their first exposure to a peer with autism can be very frightening; for others it is very exciting. It is important to answer any questions that other peers have honestly and in language appropriate to their age and level of understanding.

Behavior Management

Don't be surprised if your child begins having behavior problems once he starts school, even if he is typically cooperative. The complexity of the demands that occur in a school setting and the teacher's lack of familiarity with your child can trigger these problems.

The best way to deal with potential behavior problems is to be proactive in anticipating difficult situations. When your child starts school, the classroom staff members need to make that setting an attractive and rewarding one for him. The activities should be interesting and within his grasp and there should be an effective motivational system. He needs to experience considerable success in the early stages of the transition. For that to occur, he may need higher levels of support than he is accustomed to receiving at home or in his center-based program. Some well-timed prompts (for example, to approach other children or to take his turn in an enjoyable activity) will increase the chances that he will repeat desirable behavior and receive a great deal of reinforcement for his early efforts in the classroom. Withholding this help will probably result in increased failure and frustration.

When your child first starts school, the shadow should be generous with prompts to ensure that your child's school experience is reinforcing and successful. However, children with autism can easily become dependent on prompts, so the shadow and teacher will need to minimize prompts in specific ways. For example, they should prompt nonverbally from behind your child whenever possible and use a variety of prompts, including written words and pictures. For example, the shadow might be seated behind your child and if he is having trouble finding materials in his desk, she would point toward them. If he needs to line up, she might use a gesture to stand and then point toward the children in line. Alternately, she might show your child a photo of all the children lined up, to cue him for the transition.

You should try to use the same behavior management methods at home and in school, but sometimes that isn't practical. It is the shadow's role to monitor the differences across settings and assess the impact of the different methods. For example, many classroom teachers use specific consequences for behavior problems in class. If your child can understand and benefit from these procedures, it is preferable to use the typical classroom consequences rather than the ones used at home

Often, however, a child with autism needs an individualized approach with consequences that are more meaningful to him. If this is the case, it is helpful for parents to develop the individualized plan collaboratively with the classroom teacher. It may even be possible to incorporate elements of the classroom plan in the individual plan. This will assist in the fading process, and will help your child make the transition to accepting the typical classroom consequences.

Expecting the Unexpected

For children with autism, one of the challenges in entering an inclusive environment is dealing with the diversity of situations that occur each day. Some of these events are unpredictable and some will trigger your child's inappropriate behaviors. For example, your child may have difficulty tolerating loud noises and yet be expected to attend school-wide events in the auditorium. You can prepare him for these events by practicing problem-solving skills. In the case of the noisy assembly room, for example, he could ask to return to the classroom or to sit in the back of the auditorium if he feels overwhelmed. Some of the role-play and problem-solving skills we described in Chapter 3 are helpful here.

Reinforcing Appropriate Behaviors

It is a challenge to use an individual reward system for children with autism in a typical classroom. One reason is that giving your child the reinforcers may be distracting to him and his peers. It is important to select rewards that will not disrupt the classroom activity and can be delivered in a subtle manner. It may be possible to use reinforcers that are available to all students, such as stickers, stamps, praise, extra time with a book, computer time, or getting a drink of water.

In typical classrooms, it is also very difficult for the teacher to give any one child a high level of reinforcement. For example, it may not be possible for the teacher to tell your child "good job" for sitting quietly for a length of time. Thus, the shadow should be prepared to reinforce him as often as necessary. The teacher may also consider increasing the amount of reinforcement given to the class as a whole. If the teacher allows it, the shadow can dole out reinforcers to the other children. At a minimum, the shadow should find opportunities to provide verbal attention to the other students.

If your child is receiving consequences for inappropriate behaviors, the ratio of reinforcement to corrective comments should be at least five reinforcers for every consequence, including corrective comments. That is, your child should receive five positive comments or rewards for every corrective comment or consequence. Keep in mind that reinforcement can entail many things, and can be given for many different behaviors. For example, a reward might be given when your child initiates an interaction with another child, starts to work on his own, raises his hand to answer a question or ask for help, or takes his lunch box from his cubicle and brings it to the lunch table on his own. As your child adapts to the school routine, it is important to adjust the intervals for reinforcement.

Token or point systems are an excellent way of lengthening the intervals between tangible rewards. For example, the teacher might make check marks on a pad of paper on your child's desk when he raises his hand to ask questions, and then with the fifth checkmark give him a small sticker. This kind of system can work for an entire class, not just a child with autism. Alternatively, your child might earn points for particular behaviors, such as remaining in his seat or approaching peers on the playground, and be praised by the teacher or shadow at the time, as well as earning a check mark on a small card he carries in his pocket. Then, when he gets home at the end of the day, you would review the card and give him a tangible reward if he earned sufficient check marks.

In some classrooms, natural opportunities for reinforcement can be used. For instance, children may be allowed to find another activity of their choosing once work is completed. Most children with autism can easily learn that the sooner their work is completed, the quicker they can go to an activity of their choice. This is not only beneficial to children with autism, but also is the contingency that applies to their peers.

Dealing with Behavioral Inconsistencies Between Home and School

It is not uncommon for children with autism to pose a behavior problem in school, but not at home, or vice versa. Neither is it uncommon for them to use an adaptive skill in one of these settings but not the other. When this happens it is useful to understand why it is happening. For instance, if your child is only hitting in school, it may be because the consequences for hitting are not applied as consistently in school as they are at home. Similarly, your child may answer social questions at home with his family but not with the teacher in school, or use new vocabulary from school in the classroom but not at home. This may reflect problems with the generalization of skills, the way reinforcement is being provided, or the choice of prompts. Documenting these inconsistencies between school and home is the first step in understanding why they occur. The home-school communication log is a good way to share this kind of information.

If the teacher, shadow, and parents cannot disentangle the reasons for a child's behavior problems, this is a good time to bring in a consultant in applied behavior analysis. Some behaviors require a very sophisticated assessment and it is helpful to have an expert set up such an assessment and interpret the results.

It is also important to collect good information on problems that occur in the classroom. These should be described in detail and then shared with the behavior analyst who is consulting on integrating your child into the classroom. For example, a problem in "social relationships" might be defined in terms of such things as standing too close to peers, failing to respond to another child's initiation, walking away from peers who approach, and so forth.

Some teachers already have procedures in place for taking data on children's behaviors. In other cases, the consultant can help the teacher develop an efficient system of record keeping in which the shadow plays a key role. Data collection methods can also be developed by the team of people who work with your child at school and should be kept simple enough to be feasible in the classroom while still giving the necessary information. It is important for the teacher to be honest and realistic. If she finds the data collection process too complex to be practical, she should share her concern and work toward a simpler approach.

Functional Behavioral Assessments. When a problem behavior persists over time and/or is especially troubling, the team may need to do a functional assessment of the specific behavior to find out what variables are maintaining the behavior. That is, they will try to determine what kind of unintended reinforcement your child may be receiving for the behavior. For example, sometimes stereotyped behavior is intrinsically reinforcing because of the sensory consequences, but sometimes there is an interpersonal or attention-seeking component as well. For some children, environmental factors such as being hungry or sleepy or taking medication may also have an impact on behavior problems. A careful assessment can identify the factors that are at play for your child.

As mandated by the Individuals with Disabilities Education Act (IDEA), a functional behavioral assessment must be done prior to developing a behavior intervention plan. The behavioral consultant can help design the data collection procedure for the functional assessment and analyze the data. A more comprehensive and experimental procedure for evaluating the functions of a behavior may also be necessary. For example, rather than just observing your child in class and on the playground, the behavioral consultant may set up specific situations to tease out the events that trigger the problem behavior. He might watch your child while he is alone in a room, in a group, getting attention, or being ignored. These observations might allow him to identify very subtle factors related to the behavior that are not so obvious in the natural setting of the classroom. Appendix B has several excellent references on functional behavioral assessment.

In our experience, problem behaviors often are maintained by attention or task avoidance. An example of an attention-seeking behavior would be a child who throws things off his desk onto the floor to capture the attention of the teacher. Work avoidance is seen in the child who cries whenever he is faced with a particular kind of task, such as math worksheets or cooperative group work.

Sometimes the functional assessment may show that the behavior is maintained by different variables in different settings. For example, a child might tantrum on the playground because his peers are standing too close and tantrum in the classroom to avoid work. In these cases, it may be necessary to address the behavior differently in each situation.

Often, taking Antecedent, Behavior, and Consequence data (ABC data) yields helpful assessment information. This process enables the team to examine what happened right before the behavior happened (Antecedent), the specific Behavior exhibited, and what Consequence occurred following the behavior. Many other types of data may be collected in a functional assessment. Sometimes a videotape in the classroom might help the professional get a feel for the problem behavior. If your child needs a functional assessment, the behavior analyst or school psychologist working with the team will guide these efforts to unravel the reasons for his behavioral difficulties.

Decreasing the Need for a Shadow

During the first weeks of school, a shadow can make the difference between success and failure for the child with autism. Nonetheless, from early in your child's placement, you will want

to consider how to reduce the shadow's involvement and increase the regular classroom staff's involvement. The goal is for your child to function without a shadow.

Initially, school staff may defer to the shadow and let him take primary responsibility for interacting with your child. However, it is important that the school personnel do not become too dependent on the shadow. School staff members need to learn from the shadow, so that they can take the lead in your child's education. The shadow must eventually fade back and allow the school personnel to learn how to work with your child, even if he or she feels very protective of him. Over time, shadows should become a resource for classroom personnel rather than your child's primary support person.

There is great variability in how quickly the shadow's role can appropriately be faded. For some children, this may be accomplished within months or within a school year. For other children, it may take several years to fade the shadow. After having a shadow full time for a year or more, some children require transitional assistance at the beginning of subsequent school years. They may need three months of help one year, two months the next, and one month the third year.

One very good way for the shadow to remain a part of the classroom while fading his or her involvement is for the shadow to help other children in addition to the child with autism. The shadow may be an interesting figure to other youngsters in the class. Even though the shadow's main focus must be your child, it is important to be sensitive to the rest of the children. When your child requires less help, the shadow may assist other children who are having difficulty. Many teachers are grateful for the additional pair of hands. When the shadow works with the other children, it also helps your child build independence and practice asking for assistance.

If the shadow is helping with the other children, it may allow the classroom teacher to give your child more attention. This may, in turn, increase the likelihood of your child attending to and responding to the classroom teacher. The more opportunities he has to interact with and become comfortable with the classroom teacher, the easier it is for the shadow to fade from an active role.

As with all other aspects of educational planning, the need for a shadow is highly individualized. When a shadow is involved with your child, data should be collected on all academic and behavioral targets (goals). Any differences when the shadow is and is not present should be noted. Planning for decreasing the shadow's role should be cautious, and all reductions in support should be carefully monitored. You, the teacher, and the shadow may discuss on an informal, on-going basis how and when to fade the shadow's presence, and ultimately make the discussion a part of your child's formal IEP process.

Summary

Transitioning your child to an inclusive classroom is an exciting and formidable task. Your careful planning can greatly enhance your child's success. It is essential that your child possess the prerequisite skills that are necessary to function in the environment. It is also important that you choose a school, classroom, teacher, and shadow that match your child's needs. Clarification of roles is particularly important in the classroom. The shadow must initially help your child respond to the teacher and then gradually reduce his involvement. This takes careful planning and a systematic approach.

We know that the programs we have described in this book require hundreds of hours of hard work by parents, teachers, and children alike. There is reason to be persistent, however. Both of us (MJW & SLH) know many children who have been able to use these lessons to become more social, more expressive, and more aware of other people in their environment. Those who have mastered these skills fit in more comfortably with their peers and appear to enjoy their daily lives. Although their lives are not without challenges, these skills bring them freedom to be part of the community in which they and their families live. Persistent teaching, taking small steps at a time, with tasks appropriate to the individual, make a very big difference in the life of nearly every child with autism.

Seeing your child successfully included in a typical classroom can be the culmination of several years of hard work on social and other skills. For some children, the need to work on social skills may be ongoing; fortunate others may need little or no additional formal teaching in social skills at some point. In any case, the social skills programs in this book should help give your child the foundation in social skills he needs in order to join in with other kids at school and in the community.

References

Harris, S. L. & Handleman, J. S. (1997). Helping children with autism enter the mainstream. In D. J. Cohen & F. R. Volkmar (Eds.), *Handbook of autism and pervasive developmental disorders,* 2nd ed. (pp. 665-675). New York, NY: Wiley.

Harris, S. L. & Weiss, M. J. (1998). *Right from the start: Behavioral intervention for young children with autism.* Bethesda, MD: Woodbine House.

Lord, C. (1993). Early social development in autism. In E. Schopler, M.E. van Bourgodien, & M. M. Bristol (Eds.), *Preschool issues in autism* (pp. 61-94). New York, NY: Plenum Press.

Powers, M. D. (Ed.). (2000). *Children with autism: A parents' guide.* Bethesda, MD: Woodbine House.

APPENDIX A

Commercially Available Resources for Teaching Social Skills

A number of commercially available materials exist for teaching social skills. Some of these resources have been developed for children with autism. Others have been developed for children with other developmental difficulties, including attention deficits or learning problems. It may be helpful to use these materials to assist your child in generalization of targeted skills. Another advantage of these materials is that they are often designed to be fun and interesting. Many are organized in game formats that can reduce the monotony of instructional time.

Social Skills Curricula

General Social Skills

McGinnis, E. & Goldstein, A. P. (1990). *Skillstreaming in early childhood: Teaching prosocial skills to the preschool and kindergarten child.* (1990). Champaign: IL: Research Press.

McGinnis, E. & Goldstein, A. P. (1997). *Skillstreaming the elementary school child: New strategies and perspectives for teaching prosocial skills.* Champaign, IL: Research Press.

These curricula focus on important social skills such as asking for help, waiting, sharing, and being polite. They also address issues such as accepting "no" and dealing with losing.

Walker, H. M., McConnell, S., Holmes, D., Todis, B., Walker, J.,
 & Golden, N. (1988). *The Walker social skills program: The
 accepts program.* Austin, TX: Pro-Ed.

This curriculum contains instructional sequences on a variety of social skills. Teaching scripts are clearly outlined. There is
a strong emphasis on classroom behavior.

Connecting with Others

Richardson, R. (1996). *Connecting with others: Lessons for
 teaching social and emotional competence.* Champaign, IL:
 Research Press.

There are two volumes of this series, one for kindergarten
through second grade, and one for grades 3 through 5. Targets of
lessons include communication, problem solving, conflict resolu-
tion, sharing, and empathy.

Problem Solving

Shure, M. B. (1992). *I can problem solve.* Champaign, IL:
 Research Press.

There are three volumes in this series, for preschoolers, for
kindergarten and primary grades, and for the intermediate elementary grades. Activities focus on emotions, on why/because,
and on issues such as choices and fairness.

Books with Activities

Making Friends

Ballare, A. & Lampros, A. (1994). *Behavior smart.* West Nyack,
 NY: Center for Applied Research.

This book is designed for children in grades kindergarten
through grade 4. Activities help children to become friendly friends
and tactful talkers. Other issues addressed include table manners and appropriate behavior in other settings.

Good Manners

Schaffer, F. (1992). *Manners matter.* Torrance, CA: Frank Schaffer.
This is designed for grades 3 to 7, and covers issues such as appropriate behavior on the phone, at the table, and at social events.

Social Skills

Mannix, D. (1993). *Social skills activities for special children.* West Nyack, NY: Center for Applied Research in Education.
This book addresses the skills of getting along, for accepting rules, and for understanding etiquette.

Problem Solving and Reasoning

DeGaetano, J. G. (1996). *Problem solving activities.* Wrightsville Beach, NC: Great Ideas for Teaching.
DeGaetano, J. G. (1996). *Verbal reasoning activities.* Wrightsville Beach, NC: Great Ideas for Teaching.
DeGaetano, J. G. (1996). *Interactive language skills.* Wrightsville Beach, NC: Great Ideas for Teaching.

Social Stories

Gray, C. (1993). *The original social story book.* Arlington, TX: Future Horizons.
Gray, C. (1994). *The new social story book.* Arlington, TX: Future Horizons.
Meiners, C. J. (2000). *Social Skills Books.* Laurel, MD: Patuxent Enterprises. *socialskillsbooks@Juno.com*

Conversational Skills

Gray, C. (1994). *Comic strip conversations.* Arlington, TX: Future Horizons.

Social Language

Freeman, S. & Dake, L. (1996). *Teach me language*. Langley, BC, Canada: SKF Books.

This book contains a wonderful and diverse group of activities to build language comprehension and use.

Spector, C. C. (1997). *Saying one thing, meaning another: Activities for clarifying ambiguous language*. Eau Claire, WI: Thinking Publications.

Catalogs with Social Skills Materials

Childswork Childsplay
135 Dupont Street
Plainview, NY 11803
800-962-1141
www.guidancechannel.com

Excellent selection of social skills games:
- *You & Me*
- *The Helping, Sharing, and Caring Game*
- *The Good Behavior Game*
- *Stop, Think, & Relax*
- *Look Before You Leap*
- *Think on Your Feet*
- *The Classroom Behavior Game*
- *Circle of Friends Game*
- *Communicate Junior*
- *Mind Your Manners*

Creative Therapy Store
12031 Wilshire Blvd.
Los Angeles, CA 90025
800-648-8857
www.wpspublish.com

Some materials may be available only to professionals. Large selection of games and books.

Frank Schaffer Publications
P.O. Box 2853
Torrance, CA 90509
800-421-5565
www.frankschaffer.com
Excellent selection of activity books (e.g., on inferences, critical thinking skills).

Great Ideas for Teaching
P. O. Box 444
Wrightsville Beach, NC 28480
910-256-4494
www.gift-inc.com
Large selection of language games and flashcards.

APPENDIX B

Resources on Assessing and Addressing Challenging Behavior

There is an extensive, well-developed professional literature on treating behavior problems in children with autism. Although parents and teachers will often find they can address minor or routine problems without outside help, serious behavior problems may demand the help of an expert. At our center, we work closely with our doctoral students to teach them the skills needed for translating theory to practice in addressing challenging behavior. These books alone won't teach you those skills. Nonetheless, there are times when careful observation at home or in the classroom will give you a good idea what is motivating a behavior and you can develop your own treatment plans. When your own efforts don't pay off fairly quickly in improving behavior, it is time to call in a consultant.

Publications

Baker, B. L. & Brightman, A. J. (1997). *Steps to independence: Teaching everyday skills to children with special needs.* Baltimore, MD: Paul H. Brookes Publishing Company.

Durand, V. M. (1990). *Severe behavior problems: A functional communication training approach.* New York, NY: Guilford Press.

Leaf, R. & McEachin, J. (Eds.) (1999). *A work in progress: Behavior management strategies and a curriculum for intensive behavioral treatment of autism.* New York, NY: DRL Books.

Maurice, C., Green, G., & Luce, S. C. (Eds.) (1996). *Behavioral intervention for young children with autism: A manual for parents and professionals.* Austin, TX: Pro-Ed.

In particular, see the chapter by R. G. Romanczyk, "Behavior analysis and assessment: The cornerstone to effectiveness" (pp. 195-217).

Miller, L. K. (1997). *Principles of everyday behavior analysis.* Pacific Grove, CA: Brooks/Cole Publishing Company.

O'Neill, R. E., Horner, R. H., Albin, R. W., Storey, K., & Sprague, J. R. (1990). *Functional analysis of problem behavior: A practical assessment guide.* Sycamore, IL: Sycamore Publishing Company.

O'Neill, R. E., Horner, R. H., Sprague, J. R., Storey, K., & Newton, J. S. (1997). *Functional assessment and program development for problem behavior: A practical handbook.* Sycamore, IL: Sycamore Publishing Company.

Organization

Behavior Analyst Certification Board
519 E. Park Avenue
Tallahassee, FL 32301
www.bacb.com

For help in finding a behavioral consultant, contact the Behavior Analyst Certification Board. Their website provides details on the credentials they expect someone to have in order to be eligible to be board certified. Ideally, a behavioral consultant should be a Board Certified Behavior Analyst. However, this certification process is a relatively recent one and not every capable behavioral consultant has completed the process of certification. You want a consultant who is certified, meets the criteria to be certified, or who works under the supervision of someone who is certified.

INDEX

ABOUT THE AUTHORS

Mary Jane Weiss, Ph.D., BCBA, is a research assistant professor at Rutgers, The State University of New Jersey. She is Director of the Division of Research and Training at the Douglass Developmental Disabilities Center. Her clinical and research interest center on the identification and use of best practices within ABA intervention for individuals with autism. She is also the co-author of *RIGHT FROM THE START: BEHAVIORAL INTERVENTION FOR YOUNG CHILDREN WITH AUTISM* (Woodbine House, 1998).

Sandra L. Harris, Ph.D., is a professor at the Graduate School of Applied and Professional Psychology at Rutgers. She is the Executive Director of the Douglass Developmental Disabilities Center, a program for children and adolescents with autism, which she founded in 1972. She is also the author of *SIBLINGS OF CHILDREN WITH AUTISM: A GUIDE FOR FAMILIES* (Woodbine House, 1994) and co-author of *RIGHT FROM THE START: BEHAVIORAL INTERVENTION FOR YOUNG CHILDREN WITH AUTISM* (Woodbine House, 1998).